Praise for the k

Joanna has a way of showing you things about yourself that seem obvious afterwards, but we sometimes miss because we can't see the wood for the trees. I would encourage anyone, at any point in their career, even if senior, to read this book. You'll be surprised about how the seemingly small things you're doing (or not!) have a huge impact on how you are perceived and how you are managing your career.

Annette Bannister, Managing Director, Head of European Infrastructure, financial services

Joanna has created, in a relatively compact read, some compelling guidance and valuable development gems for professionals at any stage of their career. One of my main take aways is how important it is to plan regular time to invest in my own and my team's development and then actually act. I wish I had read this book years ago but it is never too late to learn – the honesty, practical exercises and reflection suggestions will bring me back to this book and specifically the relevant chapters again and again.

Susan Spash, Partner, Blick Rothenberg

This is the guide to turbo charge your career – it's super accessible and assists you with guides for improving your skills like building your networks, presenting yourself and developing your team with such practical nuggets. I'll be returning to its insights time and time again and can't overstate how impressive and useful this will be to anyone wanting to develop their career. I'd highly recommend it.

Melanie Stancliffe, Partner, Cripps

A thoughtful and practical guide to topics at the heart of career success. *Getting On: Making work work* sets out how success in the workplace relies, in large part, on our ability to develop and manage successful relationships. This includes our relationship with self and how to maintain and enhance our personal impact throughout our working lives. Joanna has translated my experience of her as an effective practitioner into a meaningful outline of case studies of individuals maximising their impact at work. Her book provides that rare balance of a breadth of theoretical references with pragmatic tips, and is one of those texts that offers practical wisdom on page after page.

Tony Wright, Director of Administration, UK & Workplace Experience, Latham & Watkins

We know that excelling on the job, doesn't mean that a successful career will follow – but we don't always understand why. In *Getting On: Making work work,* Joanna reminds us to be rigorous in our self-analysis and hone the skills we need to rev our career engine. It's pragmatic, thought provoking and encourages self-reflection with valuable insights for everyone, no matter what stage your career.

Unette Spencer, Chief of Staff to Executive Vice Chair, Mastercard

Ever wondered why you're not progressing as you want in your career? This is a rare, comprehensive and very readable resource to help you with understanding yourself, the sometimes confusing world of work relationships and how to approach things differently. I wish I had been able to read it earlier.

Pauline Freegard MBA, legal sector consultant

In this book, Joanna shares her wealth of experience in helping people to progress their careers. There are so many aspects that you might never think of, from how you dress and the first impressions you create, right through to managing office politics and your online presence. Each section offers many useful suggestions and worksheets that you can use to put them into practice. I think anyone who wants to make the most of their career and to be able to navigate the challenges working life brings will benefit from reading the book.

Amanda Cullen, Board Effectiveness Specialist and former senior manager in financial services

Working with Joanna is truly eye opening. She is highly skilled at helping to reveal what is hiding in plain sight. In this book, she leads you through the steps needed to enable you to honestly review yourself in order to identify the personal actions needed to navigate workplace challenges and push your career to the next level.

Amber Jefferys, Chief Administrative Officer, shipping sector

What I like most about this book is how it covers so many different topics but is so easy to read and offers such simple and practical advice alongside the theory for today's workplace. It therefore gives you a 'helicopter view' of all the individual elements of working life and how they impact and build upon each other. Having it all in one place somehow makes things make sense – very often, books focus on just one aspect, which ascribes to that element disproportionate importance and can therefore be unhelpful. I like the fact that the chapters on the different topics are all pretty evenly weighted, which implies that everything matters and you can't just focus on one thing.

I found the chapter on office politics fascinating – I had never really thought about it in a positive way before!

There is definitely something for everyone in this book, from someone looking to take the next step up on their career journey to a senior manager who just wants to learn how to approach things more effectively in a changing work environment, or someone wondering whether their current role is right for them. I can see myself dipping into it at regular intervals to remind me of specific things at particular times and I know that I will take something different from it each time, depending on where I am and what challenges I am facing.

Even where I feel that I already know the theory, being reminded of it and having it explained with some practical steps for how to adapt is useful and the actions that Joanna suggests actually feel achievable. When I have read other books of a similar nature, I have often found myself feeling demoralised and overwhelmed by how big a shift I apparently need to make, whereas the actions/tools in this book are broken down into smaller, more incremental stages that encourage experimentation. I have already put some into practice – for example, the chapter on meetings and the tips on managing virtual interactions – and they worked!

Sally Ashford, Partner, Charles Russell Speechlys LLP

For all those of you who are told that your career is in your hands and you are in the driving seat, but desperately need tools and handholding, look no further. Joanna's new book is a mine of practical steps and tools that will help you navigate that journey. My personal favourites are tips for 'disagreeing agreeably' and 'navigating difficult conversations'. Whether you are looking to break the proverbial glass ceiling, navigating a career turning point or climbing the ladder at your own pace, *Getting On: Making work work* is a one-stop shop for working through personal branding and managing relationships and communication styles to accelerate your upward trajectory.

Jyothi Menon, Cybersecurity Delivery Lead, large global bank

Joanna has always presented thought-provoking seminars and workshops full of useful help and advice. Regardless of your levels of experience and seniority, she has a gift for both reminding you what you have forgotten and teaching you something new. This book is typical of her approach, providing a concise yet thorough guide to how to establish and develop your personal brand while navigating a path to career success. Easily readable, it offers helpful tips for career starters and seasoned professionals alike, with bite-sized nuggets of advice and handy exercises and section summaries.

Frank Moxon, CEO, Hoyt Moxon

Best wishes!

GETTING ON

MAKING WORK WORK

JOANNA GAUDOIN

First published in Great Britain by Practical Inspiration Publishing, 2022

ISBN	9781788603911	(print)
	9781788603935	(epub)
	9781788603911	(mobi)

This book is dedicated to my beloved husband, family and friends who bring unbridled joy to my life and to my many valued clients and business contacts.

About the author

Joanna Gaudoin is passionate about helping people to be able to navigate the workplace challenges they come across, be the best they can be at work and fulfil their potential – to help them get on and make work work.

Joanna works with individuals by focusing on their specific challenges and objectives so they can move forward from where they are, whether that be dealing with the new aspects of a role following a promotion, handling a challenging boss or building their profile in their marketplace.

She is also highly experienced at running group sessions for companies and firms, and speaking at events on a variety of topics that are fundamentally about how people communicate and relate to others in different work scenarios to build positive professional relationships.

Over the last decade, Joanna has worked with hundreds of organisations and thousands of people to equip them with the skills they need to improve their day-to-day work situations, their career trajectories and the performance of their organisations.

Joanna has experienced many work challenges herself. Previously, she spent a decade working in marketing and consultancy with some big-name companies. However, she hadn't found the right professional focus. Candidly, her professional life became a struggle and her motivation and diligence were lacking, which she knew was not typical of her personality. She wasn't sure why, although she surmised that the roles weren't sufficiently client facing and engaging.

What Joanna did realise in her former careers was that being successful involved skills that weren't being developed or talked about. Everyone needs to work with others, both internally and potentially externally. Joanna helps her clients do this well and now wants to help you do the same with the help of this book. These 'other' professional skills involve knowing how to manage your own personal impact and how to effectively build relationships – both within your own company and elsewhere.

After several months working with a career transition coach, Joanna retrained in personal impact and related topics and established Inside Out Image in 2011. She has since further developed her knowledge and expertise, which includes becoming a licenced practitioner with the Academy for Political Intelligence.

Joanna absolutely loves working with her clients and seeing people have their 'a-ha' moments so they can really progress from where they are.

Fundamentally, she helps bright, knowledgeable people with great technical skills and experience to work on all the 'other' skills they need so they can progress their careers and boost their firm's performance. These skills are absolutely pivotal to career progression.

Joanna lives with her husband and house rabbit Betsy in South-West London, England.

To find out more about Joanna:
https://gettingonatwork.co.uk
www.linkedin.com/in/joannagaudoin
https://twitter.com/joannainsideout

Contents

Introduction

Where are you in your career right now? Have you got to where you wanted? Perhaps you feel you've made good progress but have come up against a challenge? Are you feeling frustrated, annoyed, despondent, in a rut – or do you simply want to look ahead and make the most of your working life? Are you trying to work out what is next? Have you been promoted and do you now need to work on some new skills? Have you identified some development areas to be able to make your next job move? Do some of your relationships in the workplace make your day-to-day work a challenge?

This book is for you if you feel you've had a good career so far and have worked your way up through a few roles (even various careers) but are now encountering some challenges in your day-to-day work or barriers to moving forward, or if you simply want to look ahead and think about the skills you need so you can really achieve all you want to at work.

You spend an enormous amount of time at work and it is likely to be a key part of your identity. Therefore, taking the time to make it as enjoyable and successful as you can (whatever that means for you) is worthwhile.

Wherever you are at in your working life, I hope this book will be a catalyst to enable you to navigate your challenges more easily so your working days will become more fulfilling and your career can move forward. Even if what you read about isn't 100% relevant now, I can guarantee that most of it will be at some point – particularly if you work in a service business. Remember that while others can support you in your career, it is ultimately yours to drive and manage.

Most people I have worked with over the last decade or so have had successful careers. At the point when they choose to work with me, they are generally facing a specific challenge, know things aren't how they would like (although they may not know exactly why) or realise they need to broaden their skillset to continue their progression and gain a greater sense of fulfilment. This book incorporates much of the guidance I have offered to clients over time and includes some anonymous mini case studies to bring this guidance to life.

My professional aim is to help people fulfil their potential at work, be the best they can be and achieve what they want to. I love what I do and I want to help you enjoy what you do too, by developing and using your skills and gifts.

This book is about helping you to become aware of the skills you need. They may not be new to you, but if you haven't implemented them then you won't have benefited. This book is highly practical, explaining the why as well as the what and the how, so you can take action.

What you will read about in this book is just the tip of the iceberg in terms of the things I have helped thousands of people to work on. Ultimately, I want more people to engage with these important skills and know why they are important (the starting point). I want individuals to know what makes the difference and to be able to apply these skills in their workplaces.

Most of my work is with people in professional and financial services. These sectors are particularly rewarding as these bright and highly qualified individuals have often focused predominantly on their knowledge and technical abilities. However, to become more senior, a different range of skills is required, which people often don't consider until they are at that level and experience challenges in their day-to-day working life (usually related to working with others) and/or aren't making the progress they want in their career.

The difference working on your non-technical skills makes to your career

The big challenge, as mentioned above, is that most people focus predominantly on their technical skills and knowledge. This is unsurprising if you consider the usual emphasis on gaining knowledge through education to get a first job.

If you are in a specified profession then you have usually had many exams to pass and much knowledge to gain. Even if you aren't in a specified profession, then you will have had to build your technical skills and knowledge as a foundation to carrying out your role.

In every business, you interact with people, and that means it isn't only the 'what' you do but the 'how' you deliver your work and interact with others – internally and externally – that makes the difference. If that is hard for you to consider or you are questioning it, consider the last time you bought a service.

A good example is a conveyancing solicitor. The cost would have played a role, but many people will seek a recommendation and that is rarely linked to technical brilliance (we expect that from an established law firm). It is more likely to be linked to the lawyer's efficiency and communication skills.

Technical skills and knowledge alone are insufficient; you need to work on your non-technical – dare I say 'soft' – skills to progress.

Many people have similar knowledge and technical expertise, so you need to differentiate yourself in other ways.

Even if you get promoted based on your technical knowledge and skills, they won't be enough to help you succeed in your new role. The day job changes with seniority. A partner in a law firm doesn't only spend time on client work but must also manage people, be involved in managing the firm and win new business, among other tasks. Most of what they spend time on is not helped by the legal training they completed years ago.

The sooner you can become aware of this challenge and work on the necessary skills presented in this book, the better you'll be able to weather the inevitable storms and achieve greater fulfilment in your career. It will help you to pre-empt situations and be well prepared for different professional scenarios, as well as to deal with current challenges.

As artificial intelligence becomes more widely used, the people who will keep their roles will be those who have developed their non-technical skills – the skills a computer can't readily replicate.

Other people are almost always at the heart of the challenges you will face at work, whether it's a perceived personality clash, a lack of recognition, a lack of support or difficulty getting your voice heard. That is why everything in this book relates to how you show up at work and engage with others, in different professional scenarios.

You don't work in isolation: professional relationships matter. Every day, whether you are at home, in the office or out and about, you will be interacting with others – colleagues and, in many cases, clients, potential clients and other business contacts – usually in a multitude of ways.

Most of what is covered in this book involves an investment of time and, often conscious behavioural change. In most instances, there are no 'quick fixes' but by starting to work on what I cover and taking small steps, you can make significant progress.

Before you start reading

It's easy to read a book like this and feel as if there is a lot to work on – and there is.

Before you start, I strongly suggest you take a step back and do a brief Strengths, Weaknesses, Opportunities and Threats (SWOT) analysis of your career so you can identify the areas you need to focus on. If you do that, it will help you to be more focused as you read this book. There may be some elements to work on now and many that will be applicable further down the line. A staged approach is important. If you try to do too much, too soon – particularly where the work involves behavioural change – you won't get the lasting impact you could otherwise achieve.

Make some notes, use some page markers, do whatever you need to do to highlight the elements that are relevant to you so you can come back to them and plan.

Remember how much you have achieved. Everything in this book is to help you move forward from wherever you are at and build your confidence, rather than dent it. That's why I suggest you do the SWOT first, so you will have the chance to consider what you've achieved, your strengths and the value you bring to your role and organisation. Some questions you might want to consider are:

- What work situations do you find most challenging?
- What tasks or situations make you feel most fulfilled?
- What makes you question whether you are doing well or not?
- Would you want to take a step up? Why/why not?

You may want to involve some trusted contacts in your thinking – after all, we all have blind spots.

How to read this book

This book consists of three main parts. Part 1 is all about you. This is because you need to start with yourself. Often when we have challenges at work, we think about the roles others have to play. This has a place, but it shouldn't be the starting point. We need to think about how we are showing up at work and how we are engaging. A high level of self-awareness will help you significantly. Part 2 is about different working relationships and the dynamics and issues that frequently occur. Part 3 focuses on different work situations and the skills you need to make the most of those as opportunities.

The first time you read this book, I would suggest reading the sections and chapters sequentially. Afterwards, you can come back to the key elements and chapters that you feel are specifically relevant to you and the plan you need to work on.

I suggest this because most people consider their challenges to be related to other people – and they very often are. Therefore, they want to race to that part. However, none of those people operate in isolation; indeed, in most cases it is in relation or even reaction to you. I therefore encourage you to think about yourself first and to consider how you engage with your working world.

My hope is that this book will:

- Raise your awareness of yourself and how you show up in your working world. This process is important to make change happen.
- Get you thinking about what you need to consider, including the context and skills. There are some elements at which you are bound to already be proficient but there are likely to be many you need to work on.
- Give you lots of thought-provoking content and guidance for you to take into your working life and put into practice. It is only by doing this that you can improve your current situation, have your abilities fully recognised and achieve what you want to.

All these steps matter because they will equip you with what you need to move forward. This may include getting promoted, improving your key professional relationships, winning new clients, getting more from your team or being offered a new role in another company.

I want to help you feel more fulfilled in your working life and increase the value you offer your organisation.

Each chapter suggests additional thinking and exercises you can do. They are outlined briefly within the book but you can also download a more comprehensive version of each from this webpage: **https://gettingonatwork.co.uk/bookresources**.

I hope you enjoy reading this book and that it's both a catalyst for whatever action you need to take and a guide to help you do that effectively to make the best of yourself and your career. By applying what you read here, you are more likely to achieve the outcomes you want.

Part 1

It all starts with you

As you consider your career – how you want it to develop and, potentially, some challenges you are facing right now – it is tempting to look for a magic bullet and start searching for solutions around you. However, it is essential to first understand yourself and the impact you have on your own professional life and that of others.

I always say to clients that the first step to making change happen is self-awareness – understanding how you are engaging with the situation and the important role that plays. To assess this, it helps if you take a step back from the immediate situation to be able to come at it with a fresh perspective.

I therefore strongly encourage you to read this section fully before tackling the others. At a later date, you may want to dip back into just parts of it or other sections, but as a first read, please do start here!

Chapter 1

You can't help but impact others

You walk into a room… You receive an email…You answer your phone… In those initial moments, you think something about the person or people you encounter. And they think something about you.

It might sound judgemental and shallow, but humans continually form perceptions of others. It's the way your brain protects you: by taking what it has experienced and learned, and using that to inform you about the people you encounter.

That's why your personal impact is so important and why you need to consider it wherever and whenever you encounter others – especially in a professional context.

Not only does it affect how you are perceived by others, but it also affects how confident you feel about yourself. When you are confident about how you come across, it has an impact on the way you are perceived. They are interrelated. Consider a time when you caught sight of yourself in the mirror as you left for work and thought you looked good: what impact did that have on your overall confidence for the day ahead? I once heard about a high-profile lawyer who wore specific underwear on days when he had a big case. Of course, nobody else could see them, but they made him feel good!

This chapter is focused on getting you to think about the impact you have on others professionally and how they in turn impact you. It is also concerned with the outcome of this in terms of professional relationships, your day-to-day working life and your career progression.

Forming perceptions

It's happened to us all. We've spotted someone new at a networking event or a meeting and thought they'd be someone we'd rather avoid. The perception may be wrong or it may be right. The danger is that you either spend the time trying to avoid them, which impacts the other interactions you are involved in, or it starts a negative pattern if you do end up speaking to the person, as you have already formed a negative perception. This then impacts your behaviour, which they then respond to. Often this can be extremely subtle, but it can nonetheless have an impact on the interaction.

Likewise, the opposite can happen: you see someone and something about them encourages you to engage with them. In this case, if you do encounter them, you start from a more positive place.

You can see that, in an instant, the initial foundations for a relationship – or not, where there is a choice – are set. You need to be aware of your impact on others and how you perceive others, and the outcome that can result from that.

First impressions are made quickly – some research suggests a tenth of a second,[1] other studies suggest slightly longer at

---

[1] Alex Todorov and Janine Willis, *First Impressions: Making Up Your Mind After a 100-Ms Exposure to a Face*, 2005.

two, five or even seven seconds – whichever it is, it is quick, at less than 10 seconds. It's impossible for you to communicate nothing about yourself when you encounter someone else, even if someone is left thinking you are hard to read and not knowing what to make of you.

Can first impressions be changed? Yes, but it takes time. Harvard Research also says it takes up to eight positive things to happen to reverse a negative first impression back to neutral. So why make it hard for yourself?

You can't entirely control others' perceptions. How they perceive the world is affected by their upbringing, their values and their experiences, among other elements. However, you can carefully consider what you project to others by developing awareness and considering how you engage. This matters both in the short and the long term.

How people form perceptions and impressions

There are many suppositions about what is really going on when someone is forming a perception of another. One theory I found really helpful is *strength and warmth,* as stated in John Neffinger and Matthew Kohut's book *Compelling People.*[2]

The theory explains that when people meet one another, they are subconsciously considering two aspects in assessing what someone might be like to interact with: strength and warmth. Strength is about how competent someone appears to be – when we meet them, do we feel they can fulfil the expectations of their job role, for example? Appearing confident

[2] John Neffinger and Matthew Kohut, *Compelling People: The Hidden Qualities That Make Us Influential*, 2014.

plays an important role here, although I don't suggest you 'fake' it. It's about being sure of who you are, how you want to engage with people and what you know in your professional field. Elements that support a perception of strength include an appropriate dress code for the situation/job role, upright posture and good eye contact.

Warmth is all about friendliness and trustworthiness. Indicators of warmth include smiling and an open, engaged body position. When meeting someone for the first time, it is the warmth that matters most. Without warmth, others will struggle to engage, and may even shut themselves off from you if it feels risky to start an interaction. The reason why warmth matters so much is because, as much as we may sometimes not like to acknowledge it, we are emotional as well as logical beings.

Neffinger and Kohut say a good way to judge what balance of the two someone may have is to think about how someone makes you feel. At one extreme, someone who exhibits great strength combined with no warmth – for example, a very straight posture, clipped language and no smile – may be intimidating yet command respect; someone who is all warmth and no strength – for example, smiley, nervous eye contact and uncertain in language style and/or unwillingness to be definite – may frustrate you or even cause you to pity them.

Consider the situation where there is a team with which you work in parallel – perhaps they provide data to enable you to produce reports. It is unlikely that you feel equally positive in terms of engaging with each person in that team – you are likely to have a preference. This is probably due to the different ways the individual team members engage with you – so it's an emotional response.

Remember the old adage: 'People will forget what you said or did but not how you made them feel.' Often, we struggle to define exactly why we connect more easily with one person than another. It's also important to bear in mind that not everyone will react positively to you, no matter how much you work on your personal impact and people skills.

Let's be clear, though: you cannot neglect thinking about your personal impact and the effect you have on others every day if you want to make the most of your career.

I will discuss body language in more detail in Chapter 3, but an example of someone increasing their strength could be a more alert posture and owning their physical space to a greater degree. How people respond to another person or situation varies: some of my clients say that when they are faced with an intimidating person, they increase their strength, while others say they increase their warmth, almost to try to 'charm' the other person out of their strength.

Remember that coming across as intimidating doesn't necessarily mean the person is arrogant or feels superior; it could be a front for nervousness and anxiety. You always need to be aware of the perceptions you are forming, as they may not represent reality. It could be that your feeling of intimidation is being driven by the person's perceived 'importance' – such as their job title – and your lack of confidence in a given situation, combined with how they personally come across. Which is playing the greater role in leading to a feeling of intimidation?

It is essential to remember that, while generally a balance of strength and warmth is beneficial, in certain situations a different balance is necessary. Consider the situation where one of your team is under-performing. In the first discussion, you may increase your warmth to try to understand, to get them to talk about the situation and make it clear that you want to help them. However, if you end up having the same discussion a third or fourth time, more strength is likely to be called for.

Consider these questions about your own strength and warmth:

- Where do you sit on the balance of strength and warmth?
- In what situations or with whom does this change?
- Do you think this change is outwardly obvious to others?
- How does it make you feel and what physical changes do you experience?
- Can you think of any people you know who use strength and warmth well?

> ***Resource 1: Strength and warmth chart***
> *Download this chart to map where you and key colleagues sit on it and make some notes of how this changes in different situations. Use the above questions to help you think it through.*
> **https://gettingonatwork.co.uk/bookresources**

Beyond an initial interaction

First impressions are important, particularly in situations where people don't have long to make a decision about you or you about them – think interviews and pitch meetings, for example. However, in many professional contexts, it is about so much more. It is about how you continually build on the (hopefully) positive first impression.

Mutual trust at work is fundamental. Consistent behaviour will really help others trust you because they will know what to expect from you. This doesn't mean you can't have the odd grumpy day, but broadly it means that people know how you will react and act in different scenarios. An example would be someone in your team knowing that if they approached you with a problem, you would always make time to have a discussion and work it out with them – or, if you couldn't do so at that point, you would agree on when you could. This is far better than this being the case on some days, while on other days you would fly off the handle when they approached you.

Once a solid foundation of trust is built, you are more likely to be forgiven by someone if you do slip up.

Your personal brand

Most of us are familiar with the concept of brand regarding the things we buy – clothes, shoes, household items, food, cars and more. When you think about it, what this really means is that you have associations with certain brands. This assumes the brand has done a good enough job of defining what it is about and then communicating it. It means you often quickly decide whether or not a brand is for you.

It can be about the product specifics such as taste in food and drink – perhaps you don't like the taste of Pepsi as much as you do Coca-Cola, for example. However, in many cases it is about whether you think a brand relates to you. Is it a brand you can imagine yourself buying and using?

I often cite the example of Skoda and Audi. These car brands are owned by the same manufacturer, and core parts are likely to be very similar even if some of the product details differ. Fundamentally, both cars are metal boxes that will help you get from A to B. However, if you consider who they market themselves to, it is a very different picture.

If you extrapolate this to human beings, you get to the concept of 'personal brand'. Does this mean people are objects?! Of course not. I have to confess it isn't a term I love, but it sums up the concept well. It conveys an association of personal attributes.

I ask clients to think about 'what the colleague who knows you well would say about you to the person who knows you less well, once you have left the meeting room'. As an example, 'That's Jane, she's Head of Client Service.' (The factual bit!) 'She's an extremely helpful person who is always coming up with innovative ways to make her team more effective and responsive.' In those few words, a picture has been painted.

What picture is being painted of you? Do you know how others perceive you and how they would describe you? Would you like what they say?

Personal brand is particularly important in service businesses, as many services are comparable so organisations need to differentiate themselves by how their people deliver the service. This is also why 'how' you deliver compared to others matters for your career.

A good way to summarise your personal brand is to consider which three words (which don't describe your technical skills and knowledge – I know many find this challenging!) best represent you. These words should be positive adjectives and be realistic about who you are, yet a little aspirational at the same time. These words are good to keep at the front of your mind so that when you are making decisions and taking action you can consider whether or not this supports your brand. If it doesn't, then that may be fine: there could be a very good business reason for it, but very often this thinking can help you stay on track.

So, how do you decide on your three words?

1. Start with some reflection time – consider words with which you associate yourself and the way you do your work. Try to make them words that will differentiate you – for example, 'encouraging' and 'creative' – rather than words such as 'honest', which most people consider themselves to be. When doing this, think about key career moments when you were at your best and how you worked in those instances.
2. Conduct some research among trusted professional contacts. Ask them how they would describe you (remember the words aren't related to your technical skills). When I have worked with clients on their personal brand, many have been positively surprised about how others think of them.
3. At this point, you might have many words on your list, which is a good place to start. Narrow the list down to three words. Also, consider how the three work together: they should be related to different attributes.

Resource 2: Personal brand reflection sheet

Download this sheet to help you work on your personal brand.

https://gettingonatwork.co.uk/bookresources

When you have a clear personal brand, it helps you to focus and consider how you come across to others. It needs to be authentic and genuine, yet appropriate for your professional context. When you have a personal brand that is based on these attributes, you will feel energised and it will affect how others react to you. It's definitely not about being someone else, but rather the best possible version of yourself.

Self-confidence and positive personal impact make the harder stuff easier

When you've thought about how you want to be perceived and the way you are in reality, it helps you consider what you need to work on – where your gaps are. It means you can identify when and where you are less like the best version of yourself. For many people, this is in stressful situations or when they are tired or unwell. It is only with this awareness that you can seek to consider, with greater intent, how you can improve how you come across and simultaneously increase your self-confidence in every professional scenario.

You may also want to consider whether there are elements about yourself that hold you back, and whether you can do anything about them. I'm not talking plastic surgery here, but anything that you feel you might want to do something about that would help your confidence. This is about you and nobody else at this point. I know my confidence was much lower when I was in a role I didn't enjoy. I ate cakes to comfort myself and became 13kg overweight. Losing that weight and feeling fitter and healthier definitely gave me a confidence boost. Changing roles helped too.

For you, it may be something entirely different. How you feel about and perceive yourself matters even more than others' perceptions, and your confidence affects how you engage with others.

These elements, together with the 'tools' we will work through in Chapters 2, 3 and 4, will help you to improve your gravitas and presence. Gravitas and presence may seem like lofty words that often appear hard to define, never mind achieve; however, you can improve yours. When you have gravitas and presence, it generally makes whatever you need and want to achieve a lot easier.

If you are able to have an immediate positive impact on those with whom you are engaging and to command their attention and respect, as well as their trust, much of the battle is won.

Consider a situation where you are meeting a prospective new client; if upon appearing in the room or on the video call they see you as someone that looks credible and engaged with them as an individual, they are far more likely to be open to working with you. Of course, they will need to see that you have the expertise they require and that you can provide the service they need, but if your initial personal impact was negative or unimpressive, then it will be harder to get them to engage with what you say.

Likewise, imagine a scenario where you are being put forward for a promotion. If those involved in the decision haven't worked with you specifically, they will form a perception from what they see of you in the office or in virtual meetings. If you don't come across as credible for the role, then getting it will be much more difficult. It doesn't sound fair, but if people have nothing else to inform their decision, then your personal impact will matter even more. I will come back to internal visibility in Chapter 7.

How you show up in every scenario at work matters – your personal impact matters a great deal and is foundational to the relationships you build, the influence you have and ultimately your career success. The next three chapters will look at the 'tools' you need to consider and use well to have the impact on others that you want to.

Exercise recap

Resources webpage:
https://gettingonatwork.co.uk/bookresources

- *Strength and warmth chart*: Review your strength and warmth.
- *Personal brand reflection sheet*: Consider your personal brand.

Points to remember

- Your personal impact and how you are perceived in different professional scenarios are essential to have in mind.
- A clear personal brand will help you consider how you come across and to make sure you are positively memorable to others.

Further reflections

1. How might you be perceived? On a good day? Bad day? When you're tired? When you're stressed?
2. How frequently do you consider the way you are perceived by others? How could you remember to do this more frequently?

3. How do you want to be perceived? Does this vary? Consider different situations that are relevant to you – examples include having a performance conversation with a junior team member, presenting a proposal to the senior team, or meeting a potential new client.
4. In what situations do you want or need to feel more confident? What would help you to personally feel more confident?

Chapter 2

What you wear matters

Appearance – what you wear, your clothing, how much it looks like you have bothered – however you wish to put it, this has a huge effect on your personal impact. It might sound superficial; after all, why should what you wear or the detailed aspects of your appearance matter? Surely as long as you do your job well, that's all that counts?

However, the simple truth is that it does matter – indeed, it has a huge effect on others' perceptions of you when you are physically visible, whether that be in person, on a video call or even in your LinkedIn photo. Mary Lynn Damhorst determined in 1990 that in studies, 81% said that dress communicated someone's competence, power and intelligence, while nearly 67% said it also communicated character, sociability and mood.[1] Damhorst states that 'dress is a systematic means of transmission of information about the wearer'. A person's choice of clothing can heavily influence the impression they transmit and is therefore a powerful communication tool.

If you are sceptical, think for a moment about your own expectations. If you needed to go to court as a witness and the judge sat there in a dirty, scruffy t-shirt, would you not think it unprofessional? Would you not think the judge lacked

[1] Mary Lynn Damhorst, 'In search of a common thread: Classification of information communicated through dress', *Clothing and Textiles Research Journal*, 8(2), 1–12 (1990).

the authority and presence for their role in the proceedings? Would it be different if the t-shirt were clean and newer but still a t-shirt?

If you consider this scenario, you will see that linked to what I explained in Chapter 1, the judge would be making you doubt their credibility from the start as they hadn't considered their personal impact.

It might not seem fair, but your brain reaches quick conclusions. When we see people, we are most likely to be impacted by the visual aspects – what they wear and their body language. The way they speak will also play a role. As the encounter continues, behaviour and what people say are also likely to become important parts of how we perceive someone and what we understand about them. When I ask in workshops what people first notice about others when they meet them, each person typically says something very different, but what other people wear always features.

The aim of this chapter is to help you think clearly about the role of your appearance in terms of the impact you have on others and the key elements to consider.

Greater personal judgement is now required

Forty years ago, the lines were clearer – in a professional office environment, everyone would have been wearing suits and, in the case of men, ties. It made it easy, if highly unimaginative, to get dressed for work every day. Thankfully, times have changed and we now have greater flexibility and choice. There is far more opportunity to bring in some personality and more ways to be positively memorable.

The challenge is bigger, though, as the golden rule now is 'appropriateness'. What this really means is that every day you have to make a judgement call about what you need to wear, depending on the day ahead – the planned and the unplanned.

The first consideration in a hybrid working world is whether you are in the office or not – how much of you will be seen?

The next is what you are specifically doing on a given day. The way you dress if you are going to a board meeting or speaking at an event is likely to be completely different from turning up to your team meeting.

I say 'is likely to be' as, of course, your company or firm may have a certain dress code or established norms that you want to stick to – or you may have a personal work style that doesn't vary much from day to day.

Another consideration relates to other people. The first is who you are meeting, so you need to consider how they will be dressed and how they will expect you to be dressed – particularly if they are a client.

The final consideration – which is no less important – concerns you. Consider how you are feeling on a given day and what will help you to perform to the best of your abilities. Some people are affected more than others by what they wear. Some claim that the way they dress has no effect on them while others feel more confident and focused when they wear certain types of clothing.

Comfort is the main aim for some people, while others don't feel like they are at work unless they wear certain types of clothing. I have heard of some people who have specific clothing, even if it is underwear, that they wear for important professional occasions to help their confidence.

Always consider your plans for the day and the people you are likely to encounter to help you decide what impact you need and want to make, and what type of clothing will help you achieve that. We've all turned up somewhere and felt over- or under-dressed – it's not a good feeling. I'm sure you can remember how uncomfortable you felt and how that impacted the way you engaged with people.

Equally, being inappropriately dressed can be a distraction in a professional environment. You want people to focus on what you are saying and the value you are bringing to the work, rather than what you are wearing – which is more likely if you have misjudged what is appropriate.

'Good clothes make you notice the person,
not the dress.'
– Coco Chanel

Dressing appropriately for your day

I'm sure you have a clear idea of what very formal and smart looks like but outside of that it can become less clear-cut. It's worth keeping some principles in mind that relate broadly to how authoritative versus how approachable you want to appear. It's not all or nothing, though; very often, in the current professional world, it is a blend of the two.

If you need to look more authoritative, try wearing neutrals such as black, brown, navy, white or cream and grey to increase the formality of your outfit; in particular, combine very dark and very light clothing, such as black and white. More structured clothing, which gives you more of a defined shape, is also more formal, as is plainer clothing – an absence of patterns and details such as different-coloured buttons.

An easy way to remember this is to think about what a typical UK police officer wears – black and white, no patterns, structured clothing.

To come across as more approachable, the opposite choices will help you. This means more interesting colours such as reds, blues and greens (combined with at least one neutral), less structured clothing and more patterns.

Remember that you can combine elements from both authoritative and approachable dressing guidance to communicate what you want and need to.

Resource 3: Impact reference table
Download this simple reference table of authoritative and approachable dressing guidance.
https://gettingonatwork.co.uk/bookresources

It's all about what your day has in store. If you are in the office, you may need to consider what unplanned meetings could occur. Might you be asked to come to an important last-minute meeting with a client? If so, you don't want the awkwardness of being completely inappropriately dressed. If your office dress code is more relaxed, it's worth considering what you can keep at the office that can smarten up an outfit. This may simply be a jacket, a scarf or a different pair of shoes.

Clothing choices that work for you

It's not just about others. As we discovered earlier, it's about you too. Think about what makes you feel and look good. I know I have certain 'go to' dresses when I speak at an important event or run a masterclass for a new client.

Wearing what suits you physically is also important. As we learnt earlier, you don't want people to be distracted by your clothing. If it doesn't suit you, then that's what will happen. The key considerations are the shape and fit of clothing and the colour. If I wear white, it draws the entire colour from my face and I look ill. Likewise, if I wear something very bright, it overpowers me.

Next time you're at the shops looking for clothing, try something different. Pick out some clothing of very different colours, such as dark/light and brighter/more muted, then put them up to your face. You will see that some work better than others. Of course, if you love a colour and feel good in it, you may choose to wear it even if it isn't the most suitable. Ultimately, you want to aim to draw attention to your face, which wearing the most suitable colours for you will achieve. If you trust the shop assistant, ask their opinion too.

Going back to shape and fit, this is all about clothes looking like they are yours and that they are current – that is, not those you wore when you were 6kg lighter or heavier. Check that the clothes fit you well, with no pulling or gaping, and that they are the right shape for you.

Once again, ill-fitting, ill-shaped clothes that don't work for you will attract attention to the wrong parts of you and distract from what you are saying. Often, these sorts of clothes will be uncomfortable too, and if you spend the whole meeting pulling an item of clothing back into place, this will affect how you feel, as well as distracting others.

Take time to look at your wardrobe and discard anything that looks worn out, doesn't fit or doesn't make you feel good.

A further consideration regarding colour is how visible you need or want to be. If you are the speaker at an event, and therefore people are likely to want to find you afterwards, or if you are in an important online meeting with a lot of people and want to stand out, then a statement colour is a good choice. Unless you need to be very authoritatively dressed (rare nowadays) then wearing only neutrals will help. Needing to be seen easily was apparently the reason behind Queen Elizabeth II's often-bright colour choices.

As you become more senior, having a unique personal style can help you be more memorable. Take some time to consider what that might be – look for inspiration in shops, online and in magazines, if that will help. It doesn't mean you have to always wear the same outfit in a different colour or the same colour, but rather that you develop a style that suits you, and that works for you and your professional life.

At the other end of the age spectrum, you want to avoid looking too young and too 'safe'. For instance, in a professional services firm, many juniors wear a simple black suit and white shirt on their first day – which means it's not a good choice for more senior people. You never want your clothes to be the main focus, but if you get your dress right for what the other person expects in a given situation – the sector in which they work, the type of meeting, where you are meeting and your role – they are more likely to focus on what you say.

Detail matters

Coming back to the question I ask people about what they notice about others, there are always some interesting elements on the list and smaller details never escape notice – things like decent-looking shoes, clean nails and, dare I say, well-managed nose hairs! The point is that different people notice different things and the totality of how you present yourself affects your impact. A lack of attention to detail can undermine the effort you have made in other areas, so ensure you have these elements in mind too. If you don't, it can look sloppy and as if you haven't bothered.

Even if casual dress is more appropriate for your day, the detail matters. Details can make or undermine the rest of your appearance, no matter what the dress code may be.

Of course, appearance is just part of the visual impact you have, and in the next chapter I will cover the other extremely important visual aspect: body language.

Exercise recap

Resources webpage:
https://gettingonatwork.co.uk/bookresources

- *Impact reference table:* Download the simple reference table of authoritative and approachable dressing guidance.
- Look at your wardrobe and discard anything that looks worn out, doesn't fit or doesn't make you feel good.

Points to remember

- It may seem superficial, but your appearance makes a difference to how you are perceived.
- The key challenge is to be appropriate for who you are meeting and where, and the context of the professional situation.
- You need to look and feel good to be confident and be positively memorable.

Further reflections

1. Get into the habit of thinking more about your work outfit each day (it will get easier and quicker with time). Consider what you have in your diary for the day. How do you want to be perceived? Thinking about strength and warmth will help – greater warmth is likely to mean looking more approachable, more strength is likely to involve a more authoritative look. It's not all or nothing, though!
2. How confident do you feel in the clothes you wear to work? Is it worth spending some time identifying items that you either don't enjoy wearing and/or you don't think really suit you? Charity shops are always grateful for them.
3. How could you make some less interesting work outfits more interesting?
4. Do you also need to think about other details of your appearance? Consider whether this could help your confidence as well as your outward appearance.

Chapter 3

The power of body language

A twitch of the lip... A momentary raised eyebrow... A shuffle in your chair... Even when you are not speaking, if others can see you – whether in person or on a screen – you are communicating via your body.

Likewise, you can often get an indication of what others may be thinking or feeling by what you can see of their face and body. Research shows in a face-to-face meeting that most human communication takes place through body language. Humans have an innate ability to read body language but, like many things, the strength of this ability varies between people. This is partly why I used the word 'can' when talking about you reading others.

You also need to consider the whole person when considering body language, not just one element, as that can lead to misinterpretation. For example, if somebody has their arms crossed, we all know that is a typical sign of defensiveness – but it can also mean the person is feeling cold, or perhaps it is just a habit. To lessen the chances of incorrect interpretation, you need to consider all the elements of body language that you are seeing, rather than taking meaning from just one. In this example, that means looking at the person's posture and their expression, not just their crossed arms.

It is easier to read body language when you know someone well, as when something is different it gives you more of a clue; it is more difficult to judge with new people, as you won't know what their 'norm' is.

It is, of course, possible to read body language incorrectly; you might be more vulnerable to such a judgement in a high-pressure situation – for example, if you are proposing a project to someone more senior and you are not confident they will agree. In this instance, your brain is likely to look for signs of what you expect. This means you may easily interpret incorrectly from what you see, in line with the outcome you expect, rather than the reality. This tendency happens in lots of scenarios and is called *confirmation bias*. The online Oxford Languages Dictionary defines this as 'the tendency to interpret new evidence as confirmation of one's existing beliefs or theories'.[1] It can happen in positive situations too, and still prevent you from seeing the reality.

The other 'warning' required regarding body language concerns cultural difference. This book is based on a Western perspective – although, of course, there are some cultural nuances within that sweeping area of geography.

In the first chapter, I talked about the importance of consistency regarding your personal brand and how you deal with others. This also applies to body language and language. If you are saying one thing but your body language is communicating something different, it is the body language that others will believe – whether consciously or subconsciously.

[1] Oxford Languages Dictionaries, https://languages.oup.com

I'm not suggesting you would outwardly lie, but everyone has had to stand up at work at some point and put forward something they are unsure about. The danger is if that uncertainty is communicated through your body language, then the people receiving the information won't be convinced about it either. Often, you need to 'manage' your body language as conveying exactly what you are thinking may be unhelpful at that point in time.

This chapter is all about the importance of body language for your personal impact and how you engage with others; it also covers the key elements you need to bear in mind.

The key body language elements to consider

Entire books have been written about body language; I want to outline the key aspects that I have seen really make a difference in the work I have done with clients over the years.

Resource 4: Body language elements sheet
Download this sheet which captures the key body language elements detailed below so you can make notes on what you observe about yourself and what requires most thought.
https://gettingonatwork.co.uk/bookresources

Body language needs to be definite. The minute it looks hesitant or uncertain, you are decreasing your strength (see Chapter 1) dramatically. When someone is twitchy or moving in an uncertain way, that person doesn't appear confident, which means others are likely to see them as less credible.

People too often only think about their body language when a professional situation, such as a meeting, has officially begun. However, you need to think about what you are communicating from the first second someone sees you. For example, if you are going to someone's office to meet them, might they see you out the window? Might you bump into them going in after they've gone to get a coffee or popped out to their car? Remember that perceptions are formed quickly, so from the moment someone encounters you it is worth considering the first point at which you may start projecting something about yourself to people.

Posture

The first body language element I want to cover is posture, and the way you use your body in the space around it. If you think about it, another person's posture communicates a great deal to you. This is because – unlike someone's facial expressions – it is visible from a distance. You can potentially interpret someone's frame of mind by how they stand in a doorway at a distance.

A more erect posture, whether seated or standing, communicates increased confidence and credibility. Consider the different impact someone with that posture has on you versus someone who is slightly slouched or bent over, which can be interpreted as a lack of confidence and a feeling of negativity. Posture is a personal challenge for me; the easiest way for me to keep it in check is to imagine a string coming out the top of my head, pulling me up like a puppet.

How you move

Likewise, movement can communicate a great deal to those around you, so it is important to get the balance right. While moving at a relatively quick pace is likely to make someone appear dynamic, focused and confident, if it isn't definite then it can communicate nervousness and anxiety. If a person's movement is too fast, it can make people feel they have no time for others and/or communicate that they are stressed – the precise interpretation will depend on the rest of their body language.

Slower movement is likely to lead to an interpretation of reticence and lack of confidence, so considering how you move and adjusting to different situations and people are key.

If you manage and lead others, then always walking too quickly and definitely, coupled with not taking enough time to listen to them, can make you seem unapproachable, which is not a desirable characteristic. To manage and develop people, you want them to respect you and you need to develop a sense of authority. However, at the same time you don't want challenges and questions to be buried until they become bigger issues because you appear unapproachable.

My client Gaby[2] is extremely dynamic and action orientated. She is an extrovert who loves to engage with people and get things done. One of the first things I observed about her was that everything she did happened at a fast pace – speaking, walking and even her gestures. She had experienced some challenges engaging with her colleagues – both her quieter boss and some of the people she managed. We discussed how this way of being may be making her appear unapproachable to her team and could mean senior people might feel she didn't listen and engage with them sufficiently. It came across

[2] All names related to the mini case studies have been changed for anonymity.

as if she was always in a rush, which some people struggled to engage with.

This required us to look at which specific elements she could consciously slow down and what techniques she could use to come across as calmer. Slowing her speech and pausing more frequently were obvious starting points. Doing this can be hard for some people, but remembering that others need time to consider what you are saying can be helpful to keep in mind.

Another aspect we looked at was getting Gaby to simply sit back in her chair more frequently in meetings, only leaning forward when she had something to contribute.

Imagine for a moment the impact on you if someone constantly leans forward in a meeting. It almost feels intrusive. If you sit back, it is less intimidating for people and doesn't communicate impatience and eagerness to speak all the time. This then gives others a feeling of space to contribute their points and thoughts. It also gives the option of leaning forward when you do want to contribute.

The important additional advice for Gaby in relation to this changed action was to use other body language cues – such as expressions, eye contact and gentle nodding as appropriate – to ensure people realised she was still engaged.

Owning your space

Owning your space is the other aspect that needs to be considered here. If you look as if you are trying to decrease the amount of space you occupy, it is likely to be interpreted as a lack of confidence and credibility. The main ways people tend to do this is by making themselves smaller by crossing their arms and, if standing, their legs – which then causes wobbling, and erodes a definite position. In a seated meeting, it can be slouching and holding arms close to the body or folding them.

Remember that some adaptation will be necessary. For instance, if you are the one presenting in a meeting, you may choose to increase the space you take up even further to improve your presence and gain command of the room. You may then soften your posture slightly and reduce the space you take up, to a certain degree, once you move into taking questions and discussing what you have put forward. Context is king.

Smiling

In Western culture, smiling is a great and important professional ice breaker. It helps to communicate that all-important warmth discussed in Chapter 1. Start by thinking about how much you smile. Without over-thinking it, you need to make sure smiling is appropriate in terms of timing and quantity.

I worked with a very knowledgeable and experienced compliance director, Bob, who had a lot of in-depth experience and knowledge. He smiled constantly during the initial mock interview we did. I advised him to smile slightly less as it affected his credibility. As it is not usual for someone to smile continuously, people can become suspicious that it isn't genuine, or it may even be a distraction.

Eye contact

I'm sure we have all experienced someone who avoids eye contact or who tries to make it but then averts their eyes again quickly. If you think about how this makes you feel for a moment, most of us would probably say it is somewhat disconcerting and awkward.

There is something about the eyes. When we look into someone else's eyes, we feel we connect more with the person and engage with them more effectively. Overall, we should be aiming to look someone in the eye 50–70% of the time in a one-to-one conversation. It would be odd if it was 100% of the time, as naturally in a meeting you may be checking your notes, making notes or looking generally around the room (including potentially at other people, if they are involved).

Hopefully, it goes without saying that getting your phone out mid conversation is to be avoided, unless you are clearly checking something relevant to the discussion or you explain that you need to check for a specific reason, such as an urgent email or other message. If you don't do this, it can communicate to the other person that you are bored and disengaged.

Of course, if the other person does struggle with eye contact then you can reduce yours slightly so they don't feel stared at. In most instances, as a relationship improves, those who struggle with eye contact are likely to get more comfortable with it. Not looking people in the eye during an important meeting will negatively impact your own confidence and your credibility.

In some cases, a lack of eye contact can even make someone disbelieve what you are saying. You don't want this to be the case, especially in a professional environment. In a meeting with many people, eye contact is a key way to keep even those who are saying less feeling involved and engaged. If you are presenting, then looking around the room and attempting to make eye contact is really essential to keeping people engaged.

Hand gestures

Do you use hand gestures? Without some thought, you may not actually be sure. Next time you are explaining something in a meeting or a presentation, make a note of whether you do or don't. Hands can be challenging and, certainly in situations where you feel nervous, you will notice them more. Specifically, you may wonder what to do with them.

Gestures can be a positive behaviour for several reasons. Firstly, using them helps you to take up more space, which as I said earlier is positive. Gestures also make you look confident, as you are backing up what you say with some movement. The final main reason is that movement helps to engage people more than speech alone. This is because the movement is another way to keep people's interest stimulated.

Gestures can also be a great way to show the progression of what you are saying. This might mean moving your hand(s) from left to right across your body as you recount something in order to illustrate the progression of what you are saying. It could also mean using your fingers to illustrate the number of points you have to make and holding up the requisite number of fingers as you progress through each point – this is particularly effective in interviews.

Always avoid gestures coming above your shoulders, as this is overly dramatic and can be seen as aggressive, particularly in person. You also want to avoid using gestures that appear to hurry people when this isn't required – whether that be a hand rolling forward as they speak or a constant nodding of the head, as opposed to an occasional nod of the head to demonstrate listening.

Facial expressions

You can produce many different facial expressions, although in reality you will have some you use frequently and those around you at work will probably learn to read them. Expressions communicate your feelings rather than facts, so this is an element of which you need to be particularly aware in terms of concealing certain feelings at specific points in time.

Consider someone in your team who is explaining how they approached something. You probably don't want to show confusion or disagreement until they have finished explaining fully; otherwise this is highly discouraging and is likely to prevent them from continuing to explain to the best of their ability. Therefore, you may need to actively consider your facial expression and modify it if necessary.

Some expressions are hard to control; these are called micro gestures and they involve something that happens pretty much involuntarily, such as blushing or a mouth twitch. It is extremely difficult to have command over these if they apply to you, but it can be helpful to observe them in others. After all, if the key person you need to influence in a meeting is showing signs of disengagement or disagreement, being able to deal with that is essential.

If you think someone is becoming disengaged or is not in agreement, it is important to try to deal with that; otherwise it may lead to additional challenges outside the meeting. How you do this depends on the context and the relationship you have with the person; however, possibilities include making sure you are pausing and leaving space to speak, inviting people's comments or questions or, if relevant, referring to something related to that person to engage them. Asking them a direct question at this point is a risky strategy as it can make them feel put on the spot. Following up with them one to one after the meeting can also be a good move.

It is worth considering how expressive you are and whether you think you tend to give a lot away with your facial expressions. Being aware of that and controlling the expressions you use will help you engage well with people. Your resting face is particularly worth considering to see whether it is conveying things that you don't want to convey and which may not be true, such as anger or boredom. Try to capture in the mirror your natural expression when you aren't particularly thinking or feeling anything.

A note about virtual body language

The downside of online meetings is that there is far less body language visible, and when you are meeting with more than one person, you can't see their faces in detail. Everything I said earlier about movement is pretty much lost on screen. That said, if you are fidgeting and twitching, it is visible on screen and best avoided. Staying grounded in your chair rather than moving around is just as important online as in any face-to-face meeting. If you can, avoid showing just your head – have a bit more of your body visible and, where possible, allow your hands to be seen so you can utilise hand gestures.

Eye contact can be very hard virtually, as looking at the person and trying to see their reactions rarely correlates with looking at the camera and giving direct eye contact. Try to balance this, although people do understand this about online meetings.

My final suggestions about body language are to make any movements deliberate and to be aware of any annoying mannerisms you have that may distract others from what you are saying. (I've seen some great ones, including a former colleague who used to put his thumb on his nostrils and his forefinger on the bridge of his nose when he was listening to you – try it!)

When meeting someone in person, consider 'mirroring' them – not copying each gesture, but rather sitting/standing in a similar way to facilitate the conversation. Importantly, ensure your body language is congruent with what you are saying; otherwise it may create confusion and remove credibility from your words.

Remember how effective body language is when it comes to reading others and to changing what you want to convey, whether that be credibility through stillness or excitement/passion through quicker yet still deliberate movements and expressions.

Exercise recap

Resources webpage:
https://gettingonatwork.co.uk/bookresources

- *Body language elements sheet*: Download this sheet which captures the key body language elements detailed in this chapter so you can make notes about what you observe about yourself and what requires most thought.

Points to remember

- Body language is a key way to communicate when we can see one another.
- Body language is not only important for your own communication, but also for understanding others better.
- Consider all the key body language elements rather than one or two in isolation when 'reading' others.

Further reflections

1. Spend some time deliberately looking at others' body language – newsreaders and other presenters, your colleagues, and your family and friends. What do you notice? Which elements of non-verbal communication do they use and what do they convey?
2. Consider what you communicate. How does that change with different situations? Without being inauthentic, which elements of body language mentioned above do you need to actively manage more? In which situations?
3. Ask a trusted colleague for some feedback on your body language.

Chapter 4

What you say and how

A pause... A slight deepening of tone... An increase in pitch... How you say something matters – in fact, it can totally alter the meaning of the words you say. Consider the impact on you of how someone asks you to do something in your daily life. Of course, there is the context of the who, when and what, but the how can make us perfectly happy to do whatever it is or lead us to ask 'Why should I?'.

Of course, your voice always matters whenever you are using it, but even more on the phone when others can't see you. Together with your words, it is the only personal impact 'tool' you have in that situation. If you consider ringing a call centre to make a complaint, the voice of the person who answers can give you great confidence that they are going to resolve your issue or make you feel like it will be a battle.

Without visual cues, you are forming a perception based solely on that person's voice; whether that becomes the reality is a different matter, but you may change your approach depending on that person's voice and that will also influence the outcome. This might not be fair, but it does happen.

In this chapter, we will consider in more detail why your voice matters and what you need to consider.

Volume

When considering what really makes a difference to your voice, several key factors come into play. The first is volume – quite simply, whether or not you can be heard. If you are a naturally soft-spoken person, you will have to work harder not only simply to be heard, but to convey confidence and authority, when needed.

Speaking too quietly can send a message that you don't feel confident about what you are saying – that you don't think it deserves to be heard. And if you don't think it's important, then why should others? This is similar to the discussion about not owning your space in Chapter 3.

Others will often only ask you to repeat something once or twice, usually because asking more than that makes them feel stupid or rude, as they feel they should have heard. You need to have an awareness of your voice volume and work from that point.

Consider a situation where you are the focus of attention, such as the presenter to a large audience. You will need to think more about the volume of your voice (combined with other factors we'll discuss later) to make sure everyone can hear you and you have the required impact.

The easiest way to increase the volume of your voice is to breathe more deeply – this will also moderate your pace if you have a tendency to speak too fast. The more breath you have behind your voice, the more power/volume it will have. Many people breathe too shallowly most of the time. If this is your challenge, spend some time practising breathing air in deeply so your abdomen fills out to the side, then decreases again as you exhale. This increased breath will give your voice more power – think of it like a battery at full power rather than one that has been used for several months.

Pace

This is the biggest challenge I see among all my clients, even very senior ones, when we are considering their personal impact and/or presentation skills, particularly public speaking.

Many people speak far too fast; they forget that what they are saying is unlikely to be new information to them but in many instances it is new to the people with whom they are sharing it. Speaking too quickly can make you look nervous, as if you don't want to give your words the time they deserve – or, if combined with a different set of body language, it can appear arrogant, as if you don't have time for the person or people with whom you are engaging.

My client, Paolo, worked in a large bank in London. He was fairly senior and had a wealth of experience in banking strategy. He came to work with me as he felt he was struggling to influence people at work and achieve what he needed to. He had a strong accent compared with many people around him, but he also spoke extremely fast, barely pausing for breath.

Not only did this create challenges for those trying to engage with what he was saying; it gave the overall impression that he was in a hurry and, when combined with certain body language, potentially communicated arrogance. By working on slowing his pace, we greatly improved his impact and the ease of engaging with him, as well as possibly shifting others' perceptions of him.

Pausing is an extremely powerful and important habit to get into. A pause is a particularly useful tool when you have said something that needs to really impact the listener(s) and they need to think about it in more depth. It also shows you have the confidence in yourself to leave a moment of silence. It will help you take whoever you are trying to engage on a journey with you, rather than just imparting information. We all need to breathe, so making yourself pause will help you to do this and give more power to your voice when you are speaking.

I don't see this very often, but some people go to the other extreme and speak too slowly. This can portray a lack of confidence in what is being said if the words are spoken with hesitancy. Other listeners can also get bored and disengage. If this is your challenge, the best starting point to tackling it is to think about the situations or others present that exacerbate this issue. You can then start to consider what the source of the challenge might be and to come up with potential solutions – for example, whether you need to prepare more fully or work on some of the relationships; if you feel these are weak and certain people don't rate you, that can make you more hesitant.

Clarity

The third aspect to think about is the clarity of your words. It's easy to get lazy and run words together or to just use the front of your mouth, which makes words 'flatter' and less clear. Try saying a sentence just by using the front of your mouth and then the full extent of your mouth – the outcome will be very different! This is not to say that you should apply one extreme or the other; it is simply intended to demonstrate the difference in clarity. When we are under stress, a typical response is to speed up and to only speak from the front of the mouth, which impacts clarity and the ability of others to engage and understand.

Speaking clearly is particularly important in a multicultural environment where perhaps the language you are speaking isn't the first language of all of those around you, or the other way around. If you have a strong accent that others may find challenging, you need to focus even more on enunciating your words, especially with new people who aren't used to your accent. Once again, people will only ask you to repeat something once or twice at a maximum.

As a side note, I would never advise people to work on obliterating their accent as I believe it is part of who you are and can help to make you positively memorable, as long as enough effort is made to speak at a steady pace and at the right volume, and to enunciate words clearly in order to increase the chance of people understanding.

Intonation

Whenever I ask a room of people what prevents them from listening, it is most commonly a lack of intonation. Think of it as turning a black and white picture into colour. Without changes in tone, people disengage. To help those who struggle with intonation, I recommend thinking about what you want to achieve with the audience – are you aiming to inspire them, impart information or update them? Then consider what tone of voice is appropriate – serious, light-hearted, excited. It really helps, when you are recounting something that happened or something you did, if you can imagine it or relive it in your mind as this will naturally improve your intonation.

In some languages, intonation can bring the same phrase to life as a statement, a question or a command. Consider carefully what you are trying to communicate.

> ***Resource 5: Voice elements sheet***
> *Use this to work through the different voice aspects and consider which aspects you most need to work on in different professional situations.*
> **https://gettingonatwork.co.uk/bookresources**

Language itself

Naturally, once we get beyond the quick first impression, the words you actually use have an impact and can portray a lot about who you are, your confidence, your credibility and how you engage with others.

The words you use, combined with the aspects detailed above, can convey whether you are a more assertive, passive or aggressive person in that moment – as can your relative strength and warmth. The important element here is knowing what you want to communicate. Generally, you don't want to be seen as passive all the time and being aggressive is rarely beneficial. However, there may be times when it is appropriate to be more passive – for instance, when you are not the best person to make a decision. It means that when you are more assertive, people are more likely to listen to you, so choose when it is appropriate to be perceived in different ways.

It is important never to use minimising language. A key example of this is 'just' – for instance, starting an interjection in a meeting with 'Can I just say…?' This doesn't help you appear confident about what you are about to say and is more likely to decrease others' engagement with what you say, rather than leading them to engage with it.

Often very subtle language changes make a difference. I recently changed a phrase on a client's cover letter when she was applying for a very senior position from 'I am formally submitting my application to be considered for the role of Director', to 'I am delighted to formally submit my application for the role of Director'. It's very subtle but I removed the 'consideration' sentiment in terms of being interviewed, as this communicates greater confidence. I also added 'delighted' to show some enthusiasm. It is important to consider what changes you can make in your everyday language – both written and spoken.

Another habit to avoid is stock phrases. My most detested one is 'To be honest with you'. It implies that the rest of the time you aren't being honest. Not only are many of these phrases meaningless; they are often over-used and therefore distract from what you are saying, as people notice the repetition and miss the essence of what you say. It is essential that, particularly in important meetings, you value the words you use and avoid 'wasting' any of your airtime.

Likewise, everyone uses 'ums' and 'ers' at times, but if you do this consistently then it is something you need to work on. The first step is to be aware you are doing it and then to pay more attention to when you are tempted to insert these. Where you can, replace them with pauses; this will give you time to think about what is next and also give others time to consider what you've said. There's a distinct societal pressure for speed, but very often this destroys credibility so work on the habit of giving what you say more 'space'.

Aim to be specific in the way you talk – phrases such as 'sort of' and 'like' don't really enlighten the listener very much and could be interpreted in numerous ways. Focus on clarity with the precious words you utter.

Reading others as you speak

Watch for others' body language, which may demonstrate that they haven't quite understood and that you may need to phrase something differently. An example could be a slight upturn of the mouth, a raised eyebrow or a slightly clenched face bringing to life a confused expression. If in doubt, you can always ask, 'Does that make sense?' which doesn't make you seem lacking in confidence or come across as patronising, but gives them permission to seek further clarification. People who are strong communicators will often play something back or paraphrase it to check their understanding if they are unsure.

While you will have your own way of speaking and I'm not suggesting you dramatically change your sentence construction style, it can be helpful to be aware of how others that you are trying to engage with speak. For instance, if the key person you need to engage/influence in a meeting tends to speak in a concise way and you have a propensity to speak in a more long-winded way, you may want to give this some thought. Being more concise than is your natural style may help to decrease the chance of them disengaging.

My final guidance directly related to your voice and language is to start and end strongly, whether that be when presenting or starting or closing a discussion. If you can get people's attention immediately (also helped by other elements of your personal impact), then it will make your job so much easier.

I have seen so many people communicate strongly and then, as they reach the end of their presentation, utter something like, 'So that's it really.' This doesn't portray confidence, so think about ending strongly and not just fading away with your words.

Exercise recap

Resources webpage:
https://gettingonatwork.co.uk/bookresources

- *Voice elements sheet:* Work through the different voice aspects and consider which aspects you most need to work on in different professional situations.

Points to remember

- Your voice is particularly important on the phone when there is no visual communication.
- How you use your voice plays a key role in what you communicate with your words.
- Use pauses to give your words space and others time to think.
- Be deliberate in the language you use; minimise filler language.
- Consider your speaking style in the context of who you are speaking to.

Further reflections

1. What could you work on to improve what your voice says about you?
2. Consider whether your language is inhibiting your communication. What could you work on to improve others' engagement with you?
3. In which situations is your voice negatively impacting what you want to communicate in terms of message and about yourself?

Chapter 5

Managing yourself in the time you have

All the elements you have read about in the previous four chapters have a profound impact on what you are known for and the reputation you build. However, alongside this is how you manage yourself in the time you have – which, of course, tangibly benefits your work life and the impression this creates. This is an important bridge to the next section, where we will look at interacting with others.

What to spend time on

The starting point is to think about how you manage your time, which naturally needs to start with what you need to get done. With increased seniority, there is usually a broader range of responsibilities, so allocating the right amount of time and thought to each of them is imperative to doing your role well.

I frequently see people in a new role (including those who have been promoted) struggling to deliver in all the areas they need to cover. This is primarily for one of two reasons. Often they are spending too much time on tasks they no longer need to be so involved with – particularly if they were promoted – and should leave to other people. This can happen because it feels strange and almost irresponsible to pull away from these tasks or because it is their comfort zone and something they do well. There can be some fear associated with not being involved in greater detail.

The other possibility is that they are struggling with the new elements they need to manage. This may be because they haven't considered what they are. Or, it is challenging knowing how to approach them and start working on them. In an ideal world, the transition from the previous role is easier if the new role is due to promotion in the same organisation. A good handover also helps.

If you think about it, starting to step up and do tasks beyond your role before they fit into your job description is a great way to prove you are ready for promotion. It will then make it less of a change when you are promoted. If you are finding it challenging to do this, don't be afraid to ask for help and, if relevant, request some training, coaching or mentoring to help you.

With increased seniority, many of the new tasks relate to dealing with others, such as managing people, being responsible for client relationships and bringing in new work. People often assume they 'should know' how to deliver against the additional responsibilities a new role brings – but why would this be the case? Unless someone has had a great role model in their boss or specific development then such a transition is often challenging; it is only the rare few who have these abilities innately.

One of my clients, Tosin, had worked her way up to lead her team and now needed to devote time to people management and development. She considered herself to be good with people and able to show empathy. However, there was one particular colleague who seemed to ignore what she said and argue with her at every turn. Furthermore, he demonstrated limited proactivity and wasn't stepping up into his role. She couldn't work him out, and it was causing daily friction. It was even starting to prevent her from asking him to do tasks that were a core part of his role, which wasn't fair on her or the rest of the team.

From extensive discussion, we realised that she needed to engage with him in a different way. Rather than being generally empathetic but then giving very definite instructions when something needed to happen, she needed to gently challenge him with open questioning so that he came up with a way forward himself when assigned a task so he took ownership of it. This approach was more motivating for him and gave him the challenge of coming up with an approach or solution, rather than just carrying out direct instructions. After adopting this approach, Tosin experienced a less defensive and more discursive and open team member. This meant she could delegate what she needed to and could use her time effectively.

Coming back to the challenge of a change in role, it is vital to remember that a new role should always be a challenge – but hopefully one you want! If you can do it all comfortably and easily, you are likely to get bored quickly.

My recommended starting point for managing your time well is to think about what types of tasks you need to consider. Some examples might be people management – including making sure you have the right people doing relevant tasks – as well as people development, core responsibilities (usually at a less detailed level than previously, if you have been promoted), managing stakeholders and potentially managing existing clients and business development, depending on your role. Remember that you also need to make time for your own career development. You then need to think about prioritising the different types of tasks and consider the amount of time they each require in a typical week, month or quarter.

> ***How you spend your time***
> *Spend some time considering the areas of responsibility you have, what percentage of your time they should probably be taking and what percentage they are currently taking. You can then make a plan for how to close the gap, if there is one.*

Planning your time

Once you have done some thinking and planning, a very simple method to help you allocate time effectively and to see how you are spending your time in the medium term is to colour-code your diary. Select a colour for each type of task, then apply that to your diary – for both meetings and time you need to spend working on different elements. For example, in my diary client work is purple, client prep and admin are yellow, networking is orange and personal arrangements are green.

Herein lies another important point: it is essential to block out time for any work you need to get done. If you have a role where there is a project management plan, this will be easier. If you don't, then when you have a key deadline, it is best to block out time for when you will aim to do that work in advance of the deadline. It will make your working life less stressful knowing that the work has time blocked out for it. If urgent work comes up – which it will – you won't forget anything; you'll just need to re-jig your diary to find another spot for that work you planned to do.

The other reason for time blocking is to make sure you do the tasks that might not seem urgent, but that are important. Most professionals can fill each day doing what is being shouted for loudest and, if relevant, responding to the clients directly in front of them. However, if you have responsibility for areas that may require more thought and that are more long-term, such as strategy, then you need to block time. If you don't do this, these tasks are less likely to be taken care of, which can have longer-term implications. This also applies to working on your own career.

Not managing your time well is likely to lead to more stress. Less stress not only positively impacts you directly but also affects those around you. If you are calmer and more in control of what you need to do, that will help you engage more effectively with those around you and impact the way you are perceived. Rushing around looking stressed or sounding impatient whenever you pick up the phone won't help you build optimal relationships with your team, peers, senior people and external clients and contacts. It can make you appear unapproachable and as if you don't have time to engage with them.

A good way to work is to make sure a day's work is never finished until you have a plan for the next day – what really needs to be done (and time blocked for it) and what you will do if you have any extra time. Remember to leave gaps in your day for the unexpected. This planning might sound obvious, but so few people really plan their working day.

Changing priorities

In a busy work life, change is constant, and often it can be difficult to complete what you need to as different requests and challenges come your way. This is particularly the case in a matrix organisation where the reporting lines are more varied and may increase the potential for surprise.

When a situation is changing, it is really important to take some time – even if doesn't feel as if you have much – to consider what the priorities are. Has the situation fundamentally changed with the new request or occurrence, or not?

In all likelihood, you have heard of the Eisenhower Matrix (see Figure 5.1).

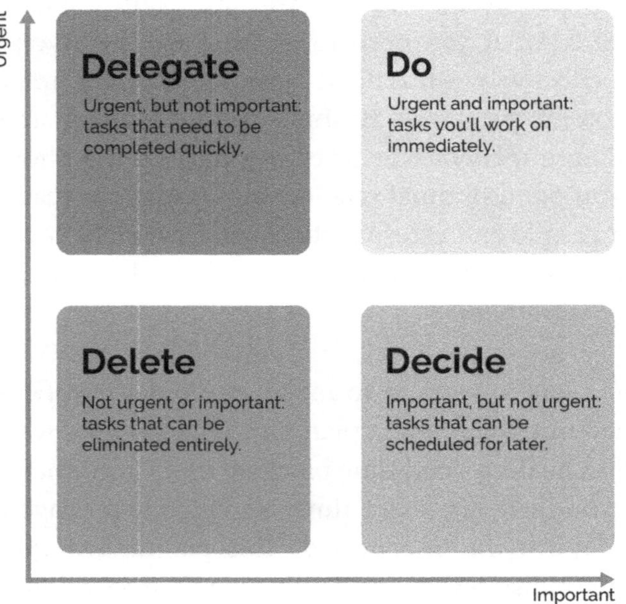

Figure 5.1: The Eisenhower Matrix

Naturally, the starting point is considering where the new request comes from and then, as Figure 5.1 illustrates, thinking about the relative importance/urgency of the new items compared with your current 'to do' list. This may involve some negotiation with others as the relative importance/urgency is unlikely to be perceived uniformly by all those involved.

Linked to this prioritisation is also avoiding being a 'yes' person. It doesn't mean you can't be seen as a supportive or helpful person, but it is rare that people in senior positions have consistently been 'yes' people in terms of doing whatever is asked of them. When you say 'yes' to a request, it means you are going to need to say 'no' to something else or have less time for other tasks. There is judgement required about whether the request should be granted. Key considerations are likely to include:

- Who is asking?
- What are the consequences of not doing this at all as well as not doing it right now?
- Am I well placed to do this or is there someone else more suitable?
- How will this fit alongside what else I have to do at this time?
- Does this present an opportunity to step up and demonstrate more senior/different skills? Is there a long-term career advantage for me?

Considering your boundaries

Take some time to consider whether there are certain people or certain situations where you need to have stronger and clearer boundaries.

There are times when you may be asked to do something as a favour – which is fine – but if it is because someone else can't be bothered or can't find the time to ask someone more appropriate to do it and there is no benefit to you, then it is not yours to accept. Be clear with yourself about why you are agreeing to something or not. Consider the difference between someone asking you to take over a task for them without any clear reason why (you suspect they want to go home for the day) versus someone asking you to take on part of the task because they are risking missing an important deadline.

It can feel difficult to decline to help someone; however, if you feel they are asking you to do something without any good reason, then asking them more about why they are unable to do it or explaining clearly and briefly why you can't help is necessary. Helping people is important, but if you are doing it too often for the wrong reasons then boundaries get blurred.

Negative 'office politics' is one of the main causes of workplace stress and absence in the United Kingdom, and there will be more on this in Chapter 9. A lack of boundaries is one of the main reasons why people end up feeling put upon. It also leads to reduced respect from others and makes it harder to get your work recognised and ultimately progress your career. It can lead to the start of a negative cycle that is hard to break without decisive action.

If you can be clear on how you manage your time and your boundaries, it will make working life more manageable (it is never fully within your control!) and make challenging situations easier to handle.

Your career is a marathon, not a sprint. With increased seniority, you will have more to balance, so boundaries and time management are even more important to ensure you don't end up burnt out. You also need to keep an eye on your team. Remember that you are a role model for your team; time management and boundaries are important elements of that.

Exercise recap

- Spend some time considering the areas of responsibility you have, what percentage of your time they require and what percentage they are currently taking. You can then make a plan for how to close the gap if there is one.
- Take some time to consider whether there are certain people or certain situations where you need to have stronger and clearer boundaries.

Points to remember

- Consider carefully the work elements on which you need to spend time and ensure you make time for them. This is particularly important to do when you move into a new role.
- Plan your time in advance, and make sure there is time allocated to elements you need to work on, not only meetings with others. Make time for elements that might not seem urgent but are important.
- When new requests come to light, consider them carefully in the context of the other work you have to do.

Further reflections

1. What do you really need to work on in your role?
2. What needs more and what needs less time compared with the current time spent?
3. Consider how easily you get distracted and what you could do about that.
4. How could you organise your days more effectively to reduce personal stress and improve the way you are perceived?
5. How could you plan more effectively to make better use of your time?

Part 2

The relationships you need

The previous part focused on you and what you need to consider as you show up in your working life each day. It addressed the areas you can consider broadly in isolation and work on to improve how you are perceived and how you engage with others. Think of it a bit like the foundations of a house.

This part will look at the relationships you need and how to build them positively, not only to make your working life more positive and productive from day to day and for your own career success, but also for the success of your company or firm.

Most of the work I do with individual clients relates to their professional relationships. This includes making a positive impact and building rapport in a job interview to get a new role or promotion, presenting effectively, dealing with different working styles, challenges with specific individuals, conflict or developing a plan to become more widely known in the workplace, among many other important topics. Often, my work with clients covers a range of challenges as it is rarely one single factor that causes someone to have difficulties or which requires focus if they are to progress their career as they want to.

I frequently remind people that none of us work on a desert island. Even when you are working from home, you have frequent interactions with people, whether that is by email, phone or video call. You need to appreciate the need for interdependency and be able to work with others positively; you can achieve very little alone.

This need for interdependency increases with seniority, when you are usually working with a broader range of people externally and internally – peers, juniors and more senior people. Your day-to-day ability to do your job and your ability to improve your career are inextricably linked to others and theirs to you. Therefore, prioritising relationships and building them well is imperative to your career success.

Humans are not purely logical beings; we are emotional creatures too – even though we might not like to see it this way in our professional lives. If you think for a minute about those with whom you have stronger relationships at work, there may not always be a 'rational' reason. It's just 'something about them', or perhaps you share similar interests and views. There might be someone who is far more knowledgeable than their colleague in a team you work with, but they are harder to work with and less reliable. Therefore, your preference is to work with the less knowledgeable but more helpful and reliable person. Many would say this is illogical.

Therefore, emotional intelligence (EQ or EI) is essential at work if you are going to maximise your potential. This means having a clear understanding of your emotions and those of others, as well as being able to manage yours. Essentially, focusing only on the core tasks of your role and not considering the people element is folly, and will not only lead to more day-to-day challenges but also stunt your career progression.

As humans, we are made to be social beings, so positive work relationships can be a source of joy too. It is often said that people leave a boss, not a job, and I see many people who leave because of other people. Companies and firms aren't negative in themselves; it is the behaviour of the people within them that can be problematic.

A lack of communication or failure to really engage with others can lead to misunderstandings and assumptions that contribute to negative patterns and cycles. Communication voids often get filled with incorrect situational interpretations.

Imagine the scenario where your line manager asks you to cover something you wouldn't usually do in a meeting. Others could interpret this as you pushing yourself forward and potentially getting involved where you shouldn't. This is more likely to be the case if there is a lack of trust and poor relationships, as well as it not being made clear that you've been asked to do this.

Considering what others don't know and how they could therefore perceive situations is key to help you consider necessary communication.

Spending time on your key relationships in order to really get to understand others and how best to work with them will pay dividends in the future, even if it feels painful and like a huge investment of time in the short term.

It is easy to say and think that a negative work environment is not your problem. It is true that it can be hard to change negative cultures and behaviours alone, but any organisation is the sum of its people. Change happens slowly and you can only change others by behaving differently yourself.

As you read Part 2, keep in mind what you read in Part 1 when considering what you need to do to improve your relationships.

Chapter 6

The foundations of great relationships

Let's face it, you won't like everyone and not everyone will like you. This is an important reality to keep in mind, even if you generally get on well with others. However, there is a lot you can do to influence the professional relationships you are involved in.

In some cases, how you engage with people initially may determine whether a professional relationship gets established at all. Think about a prospective client meeting where there is no certainty the person will become a client. This will be down to your knowledge and whether they think you can help them, but also what they think you will be like to work with – the 'how' you work.

We have all decided against using a company or a firm as we couldn't see ourselves working with a person or the people there because of the perception we formed of them. Another situation to consider in this regard is meeting someone new at a networking event, whether you stay in contact or not.

In other circumstances, we may have no choice about whether there is a relationship – for instance, the line manager you end up with. In the case of the people with whom you have to have a relationship, it is imperative to make time to work on them, to improve your everyday work life and potentially avoid any negative impact on your future career.

The starting point for relationships

The foundations of good relationships are simple: know, like and trust. However, these foundations take time to put in place; Rome was not built in a day, and nor are relationships.

Let's look at each of these foundations in turn. First, *know*: sounds simple, right? People, of course, need to know you to have a relationship with you. The reality, though, is that so few professional people make the time to know people beyond their obvious day-to-day working environment. We'll look at this more in a later chapter, but the important element to keep in mind for now is that being known at work is both positive and essential.

Once people know you, ideally they will *like* you. By this I don't mean you need to bend over backward and say 'yes' to everything others ask of you; instead, you need to create a connection with them. The essence of how you do this is simply to be human. Far too many people are so focused on what they need to achieve or feel pressure to showcase what they have been doing that they forget this.

Being human means talking about normal human topics. It might sound clichéd, but general exchanges on how the day is going (in the United Kingdom, this usually involves some mention of the weather!) or what the other person did at the weekend are important precursors to discussing work.

If you have met someone before or work with them often, remembering things about them will help a great deal. There is no quicker way to build rapport than when someone feels valued by you. The Oxford Dictionary defines rapport as 'a close and harmonious relationship in which the people or groups concerned understand each other's feelings or ideas and communicate well'.

Some people are excellent at building rapport the minute they meet strangers. Consider Catherine, Princess of Wales, in the British royal family: she is seen in many different settings and you always get the sense that she makes those to whom she speaks feel valued.

A simple way of building rapport at work is to remember what people have said – simple exchanges such as 'You mentioned your daughter was ill last week – is she better?', 'How was that boat trip you were going on last weekend?' or 'How was your son's wedding last month?'. These are very simple questions, but psychologically they make people feel you are sufficiently interested in them to, firstly, remember something from their life and, secondly, care enough to ask about it. This then creates a connection and fertile ground for relationship development.

The third element, *trust*, can be a little trickier to nail down. One way of seeing it is as having two sides. Personal trust relates to someone being trustworthy in everyday life – so not running away with someone's laptop bag if it was left with you. The other type of trust is professional, and this relates to the degree to which someone believes you are good at your job. Personal trust often comes easily if someone likes you – think about it, it is rare to like someone you wouldn't trust with your bag!

Professional trust can take more time to develop and will depend to some degree on the person who you want to trust you. For example, some people need to actually experience your work before giving that trust, while others will trust you professionally if they like you.

Trust can be fragile, but is much more robust when it is built on a relationship as well as the completion of tasks. Relationships where there is real trust are more likely to be forgiving, as there is a human connection.

Remember that underpinning all of this is your personal impact. Initial 'cold' body language and lack of engagement can greatly hinder someone even wanting to know you if they have the choice – and if they don't have the choice, this can greatly hinder likeability and trust-building!

Positive relationships and trust at work make life a lot easier in both normal and more challenging times. They help people to be more open and upfront with you, so you know what is really happening. If it isn't your habit to make time for casual conversations that aren't purpose driven with your colleagues, now is the time to start addressing this. They don't have to be fluffy or drawn out.

Particularly if you are an introvert, focus on a relationship or two at a time and start to build greater rapport one to one, rather than in groups. An introvert is defined by the Oxford Learner's Dictionary as 'a quiet person who is more interested in their own thoughts and feelings than in spending time with other people'.

More detail on building trust

To delve a bit deeper into trust building, I hope you will find this formula from the book *The Trusted Advisor*[1] helpful.

---

[1] D.H. Maister, C.H. Green and R.M. Galford, *The Trusted Advisor*, 20th anniversary edition (2021).

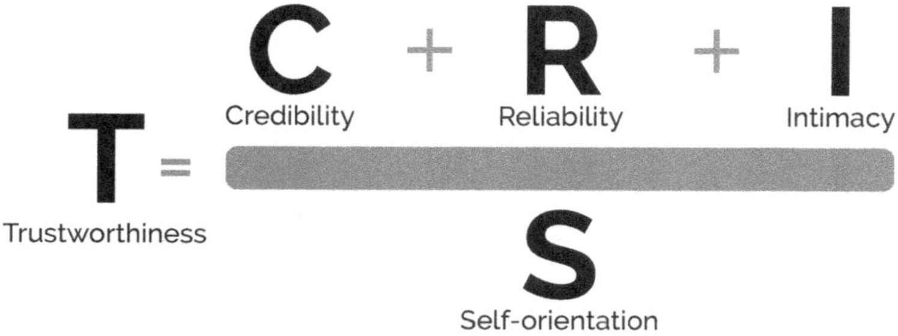

$$T = \frac{C + R + I}{S}$$

Credibility Reliability Intimacy

Trustworthiness

Self-orientation

Essentially, it says that by working on all the elements on the top line of the formula, you can greatly increase the trust others have in you. However, this can be reduced if it is obvious that you are very focused on your own goals and what you can get from the relationship or situation.

Let's look at each of the elements on which you need to focus in turn.

Credibility

Credibility is all about being believable, so that people easily believe you will do a good job at whatever it is you are saying you will do or are doing. Ticking the credibility box makes it easier to win work, bring up differences of opinion and be respected for what you do. Some of this is related to your personal impact. How credible would you consider a newsreader who was hunched over their desk, wearing scruffy clothes and speaking in a monotone voice? I think you'd change the channel or go to a different web page pretty quickly. Naturally, what you say (the expertise you demonstrate) and how you behave also have an important role to play.

Likewise, if you are positioning yourself for promotion, those making the decision need to be able to envisage you stepping up into the role.

Without being credible fairly quickly, you will have to fight harder for what you are trying to achieve.

Reliability

The second element, reliability, relates to doing what you say you will do and engaging with people consistently. Doing what you said you would is the ultimate trust builder. Think back to what you read in Chapter 1 regarding your personal brand.

Reliability takes time to demonstrate; if your first encounter is a meeting and you turn up on time, that is a good start. However, over time it means continuing such behaviour and carrying out any actions you said you would, by when you said you would.

It's about managing others' expectations. If you are going to miss a deadline, being reliable would mean telling the relevant people slightly in advance (certainly not after the deadline has passed) and providing an update on when you expect to meet it. Being reliable might sound a bit dull and hard work to stay on top of all you need to (see Chapter 5), but it greatly helps in building trust and in the long run is likely to mean you will get chased less as people know you will either deliver, or update them if you can't. Everyone has the odd slip-up and forgets to do something at times, but once a relationship is established and you have demonstrated reliability, people are likely to be more forgiving as they know it is unusual for you.

Intimacy

Finally, intimacy really refers to connectedness: engaging with people so they feel valued. This relates to what I said earlier about remembering things about people, as well as making time for 'small talk'.

Many people dread 'small talk'; however, it is essential to build rapport with someone and a relationship over time. It creates intimacy. If you start discussing the work topic in a meeting straight away, it can be extremely abrupt and strange.

Think of 'small talk' like a warm-up for the work-focused conversation. So many people aren't prepared to make the time to engage with others. Not bothering might have a short-term time-saving benefit but it won't facilitate working together over the long term. Without small talk and rapport-building, both the professional conversation and relationship are likely to be less fruitful.

Imagine someone approaching another person at a networking event and their first line being, 'Hello, so what do you do?' Could anything be more off-putting? Does anyone respond well to that question? No! People realise we go to networking events for professional reasons; however, it makes people feel that someone is only interested in them for their work persona and it feels like a very hard, cold question to start with. It can imply that the person is trying to filter out who is useful to them and who is not. Most of the time, someone isn't doing this deliberately; they are just nervous and don't know what else to say. However, it's really unhelpful for building a relationship. A comparison might be someone asking the other person how much they earn on a first date.

If you dread 'small talk' and don't know what to say, consider points of commonality – hence why the weather often comes up! Topics such as how the person travelled to the place where you met; if it's a Monday, how their weekend was; if it's a Friday, what plans they have for the weekend – you get the idea. You want to avoid personal questions until you know someone better, but these questions can all be answered generally if someone doesn't feel comfortable giving too much information away.

Some people who consider themselves introverts may find these actions more challenging; my advice is to build up your skills slowly. Increase your confidence through small actions. The initial challenge may be easier for extroverts, but sometimes they have the opposite problem and share too much too quickly, which can come across as unprofessional, not genuine or both.

Additionally, if too much information is shared too soon without knowing the other person, there is a danger that they may use it against you. Someone in a workshop once told me she'd explained to her new boss that she was concerned she lacked a certain skill for the role; he subsequently brought this up in meetings to put her on the backfoot. She felt this wasn't because he believed it was actually true, as he couldn't offer any concrete examples; rather, it was because she'd put the thought in his mind and he decided to 'use it'. It is vital to find a balance between engaging and being human, but not saying too much – especially on a first introduction or in an initial meeting.

Once someone starts sharing more personal information regarding their partner, children and where they live, they are giving you permission to ask a bit more about those topics.

Of course, if any conversation or interaction you have with someone is completely geared around what you want to get out of it – if it is self-orientated – then this will undermine trust-building. Goals and objectives are important but always make sure you don't come across as focused on what you want out of a situation, either in words or communication style.

Resource 6: Trust equation review sheet
Use this sheet to consider what your strengths and weaknesses are in relation to the trust equation.
https://gettingonatwork.co.uk/bookresources

According to a survey, Sir David Attenborough is considered one of the most trusted celebrities in the United Kingdom[2] – what is it about him that makes this the case? Consider for the moment his voice, body language and personal appearance – how do these contribute to trust-building?

The concept of trust has wider implications too. You want and need people to trust you, but you also need to trust others. This can feel 'chicken and egg' – that is, 'I won't trust them with a task until they have shown they can do it.' How can they if you don't let them? This is particularly relevant if you manage others – and it can feel risky. I'll look at managing others in greater depth later, but consider tasks you can get others to do that are relatively low risk or, if they are higher risk, break them down into stages offering suitable support and review slots so you can be sure things are on track. If others feel you don't trust them, this will negatively impact

[2] A. Molloy, 'Attenborough is named the UK's most trustworthy figure', *Independent*, 2 February. Available from https://www.independent.co.uk/news/people/news/wildlife-presenter-david-attenborough-is-named-the-uk-s-most-trustworthy-figure-9102139.html

the relationship, and in the end they are likely to stop trying – not being trusted is highly demotivating.

People are different

I acknowledged at the start of this chapter that you won't like everyone you encounter at work and vice versa. However, it will greatly help if you keep in mind that people are different. You know this factually, but it often gets forgotten when dealing with others. Appreciating those differences is valuable and has implications for how you deal with other people. Without this, you will experience more day-to-day challenges in dealing with others and you won't build the variety of relationships that you need at work, as you are likely to focus most on those who are similar to you and with whom you feel a natural connectedness.

While you do need to be consistent in who you are, you do also need to adapt your behaviour and style somewhat to different people.

In his brilliantly simple and clear book *Surrounded by Idiots*,[3] Thomas Erikson starts from the premise that very few people in the world will share the same viewpoint as us about absolutely everything, let alone react and behave in the same way. Therefore, it is easy to conclude that others are 'idiots'.

This is not going to be a helpful conclusion, though, as you are very likely to have to deal with different types of people, both internally and externally. A better approach is to work on how you communicate with people who are different to you.

[3] T. Erikson, *Surrounded by Idiots: The four types of human behaviour* (2019).

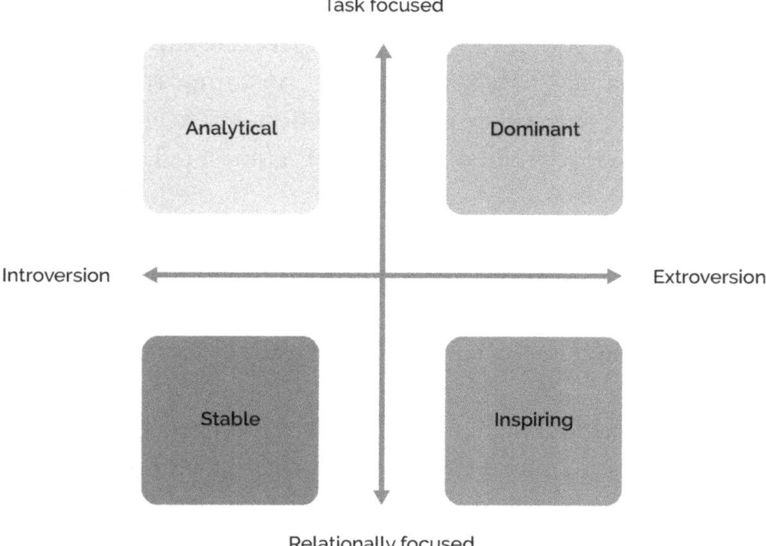

Figure 6.1: Erikson's four quadrants

Figure 6.1 shows how Erikson views different people (there are clear similarities with other models and assessment tools). Rarely do individuals 'sit' in one of the quadrants. We are all an interesting mix. Nevertheless, it is a helpful framework for thinking about how people are. Often, by observing people and how they engage, you can get a sense of where they are on at least one of the axes. You can then consider the implications for how best to interact with them.

The quadrants diagonally opposite one another are likely to have the greatest challenges in terms of engaging with and understanding one another. If you are a more introverted character focused on getting things done, you are likely to find someone more extroverted who is relationally focused 'a bit much'. This could mean physically in terms of voice volume and the body language they use (perhaps overt, dramatic gestures), but also in terms of their need to put the relationship between you first, which could feel like time wasting to you. While a task may seem like the most important thing in the moment, remember that the relationship needs to endure long after that particular work task is completed.

I would argue that even introverted, task-focused people value human connection and 'small talk'. It is the approach with these people that is likely to be different – for instance, engaging in a more low-key, less-energetic manner and for less time.

If you are relationally focused, it may be hard to deal with those who don't make time for relationships and want to get straight to the task. My most important piece of advice would be to not take this personally and to try to avoid it affecting your overall view of who they are, their competence and their ability.

The challenge is to get to know one another and to establish how best to engage with each other. If both people consider this and make slight adjustments from their usual behaviour, this will increase the likelihood of a positive outcome.

Another excellent framework that provides a great perspective on people differences is Gretchen Rubin's *Four Tendencies*.[4] This looks at how individuals respond to expectations: both outer expectations, or requests and expectations coming from others – for example, to meet a deadline – and inner expectations, which might include aims such as losing weight, working on your career development or doing more exercise.

---

[4] G. Rubin, *The Four Tendencies* (2017).

In this framework, people fall into one of four types:

- Upholder – meets both inner and outer expectations.
- Obliger – meets outer expectations.
- Questioner – meets inner expectations.
- Rebel – struggles to meet either.

It is worth reading further about this, as it is interesting to think about both your approach to expectations and whether those with whom you work may differ in theirs. This will help you to understand them better. For instance, you may be someone who never misses a deadline, while others seem to treat deadlines as a reminder to do the task. To bring the model to life somewhat, you may be an upholder and once you decide you are going to lose weight and get fit you make a plan and do it. An obliger may want to do that but because it is an inner expectation, it is less likely to happen as there will always be many other outer expectations from colleagues, friends and family so there is never enough time. That person's way of getting something to happen is to tell others and make it an outer expectation.

If you encounter a questioner at work, you may feel they don't trust you as they are always asking questions when you ask them to do something. However, asking questions is their mindset and their way of really understanding just how important what you are asking them to do is, so they can decide whether to make it an inner expectation that they commit to (or not!).

Having this lens of understanding can greatly help you understand why others' responses may differ from your own. With this sort of person, it may be helpful to ask them to suggest a deadline as a starting point, even if you then need to negotiate, rather than starting by imposing one. Rebels present the greatest challenge, as many of the strategies for the other tendencies don't work with them. It is worth reading more on dealing with rebels as they are focused more on personal identity and being true to themselves. They like to do the things they want, when they want.

I recommend you do Gretchen Rubin's Four Tendencies quiz online: **https://quiz.gretchenrubin.com/**

When you consider the range of differing values, beliefs and agendas in the workplace, you can see why adjustment can be necessary to build productive professional relationships. People have differing frames of references and views on how things should be done, so without trying to understand others better it is very easy to fall foul of all these numerous differences.

Top 10 relationship skills

I talked earlier about valuing others, and this needs to be a principle in dealing with other people. Here are 10 key skills on which to focus to improve your professional relationships:

1. Consider how you come across

As discussed in Part 1, how you come across to others has a huge impact on the way you are perceived and the resulting interactions. It is important to take the time to understand how others could perceive your demeanour, words and behaviour.

2. Demonstrate empathy

This is an important way to show you value someone and that you have taken the time to share in what they are experiencing – whether that be delight that a project has been delivered successfully, frustration at a delay or their view on an approach to a project. As humans, we want to feel understood – to believe that people 'get us', even at work. It doesn't necessarily mean that you agree, but rather that you are seeking to understand where someone is coming from.

3. Listen

As we have learned, a key way to value others is by remembering what they said. The first step to this is listening – and listening properly. It is not just about actually listening but also about making sure the other person feels heard.

Many misunderstandings could be avoided and anger quelled by people engaging their ears. Often, people spend far too much time thinking of what to say next rather than listening to what is being said. You can end up responding to the information you thought you heard rather than what was said, or leaving the other person feeling you don't value them and don't want to hear what they are saying.

Additionally, asking questions and listening can help improve the way you are perceived. It communicates that you are confident (even if you don't feel it!). Those who rush in to demonstrate their credibility and knowledge may do exactly the opposite by over-speaking; it can also appear rude and arrogant.

Verifying what you have heard to check your understanding is a good technique to confirm you were listening and to make sure you have a shared understanding. People are often too quick to rush in with solutions without having done the first key step of listening sufficiently. A frustrated and angry person will become less so if they feel heard first.

Part of this tendency to listen insufficiently comes from the pressure you may feel to get things done rapidly – the idea that an instant answer is required for fear that you don't look like you are 'on it' or you lack the knowledge.

4. Take the time to react

There is a lot of pressure to react quickly in today's working environment. This is very much the case with email: far too many emails are responded to much too quickly. The danger is that you don't read them thoroughly enough to be sure of the meaning and/or you might send a response that you'll regret later. If you read an email quickly and respond quickly after having misinterpreted it, it can set up a negative interaction pattern very quickly. Not thinking through the appropriate response and/or action to take can have significant consequences.

Taking time to react is particularly important when you hear or experience something that provokes a negative feeling – whether that be anger, frustration, annoyance or disbelief. There is absolutely no problem most of the time in telling someone you will come back to them, as long as you commit to a timeframe and stick to it.

After that, it is important to think about the reaction (feeling you had), but also focus on the outcome you want from the situation or relationship (Figure 6.2). An example might be a senior stakeholder saying a project deadline needs to be brought forward. Think about the situation in balance: whether that is really an issue, whether it is possible, the potential downsides and whether this is a stakeholder who does this all the time or one who doesn't. The importance of the relationship also needs to be considered.

You need to take all the elements into account to decide how to react. Thinking this through means your reaction is likely to be much better than reacting immediately when you receive the information. If you do go back and do battle, it is likely to land better too, as it is clear you have considered it, rather than just responding with an instant emotional reaction that hasn't been thought through. You are also likely to deliver your message more clearly and appropriately.

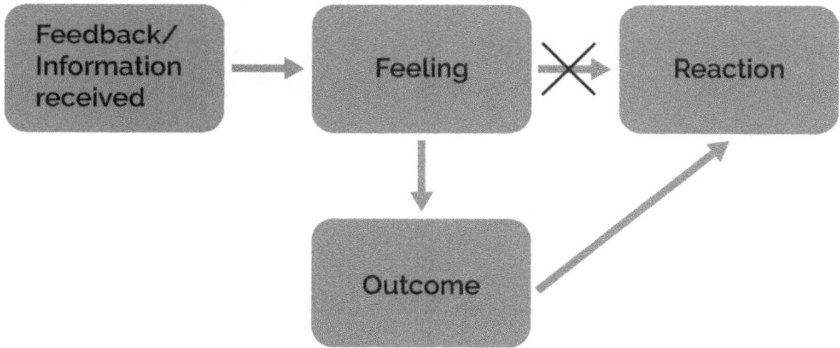

Figure 6.2: Taking the time to react

Over time, it is good practice to see whether there are any regular triggers for your negative reactions. You can then identify whether they occur in relation to specific people, which means the relationships probably need work. If they relate to specific situations, you need to uncover the root cause. It could be about a repeated frustration with the organisation or something that makes you feel vulnerable, insecure or lacking in confidence. It is only with good self-awareness that you will be able to work on developing the right element to improve things in the future.

5. Understand the perspectives of others

You need to remember that others' frames of reference are very likely to be different from yours. The challenge when you have a differing view is to ask yourself in what situation and with which assumptions or understanding that person could hold their position. Open questions are a great way to understand more without starting with a critique; this approach is also less likely to make someone defensive.

6. Show vulnerability and humility

People are often afraid to appear 'weak' at work, and often equate this with needing to put on a work 'mask'. Yes, you need to consider your personal impact and respect for others, but sharing something of yourself with people and showing some vulnerability, when appropriate, can hasten positive relationship development.

You don't have to make out you know the answer all the time. In fact, when you are willing to say you don't know, it helps you come across in a more genuine way. It also reassures people that when you are being forthright you do know what you are talking about. Acting this way helps others to be more genuine and transparent too, so better discussions occur and improved decision-making happens. As long as you commit to going back to people with the answers they need, and do so reliably, there is no issue; people will often appreciate your honesty and the time you have taken to get the correct answer. Remember the power of 'don't know'.

7. Appreciate others

It is vital to acknowledge others' contributions to make them feel valued. That may include thanking them specifically and/or acknowledging good work or acknowledging work done by others that you are passing on or presenting. No matter what you think of him, during the height of the Covid-19 pandemic, the then UK Prime Minister Boris Johnson exhibited a key positive behaviour. He periodically gave credit to others and deferred to them to respond during press conferences, acknowledging when others had done well and when they were more knowledgeable and better placed to answer a question than him.

Similarly, someone in a workshop I ran commented how the team leader, who was very senior, always made time to thank people, sometimes publicly in front of others, which she said greatly enhanced her feelings about her work, him and the bank overall.

It is important to give credit to others for the work they have done. If you are struggling to get credit for work you have done and, worse still, someone else is claiming it, then it is important to have a conversation with the person or people involved. This may involve you asking whether you can be the one sending the work on and/or presenting at least part of it in a relevant meeting. This can feel challenging, but it is important not to let people get used to passing off your work as their own.

8. Establish relationships on the right footing

'Teaching people how to treat you' is a key mantra of *Gravitas* author Caroline Goyder,[5] and it is a vital skill at work. It involves having boundaries in all sorts of areas. Constantly trying to please an awkward person is rarely going to stop them being awkward; instead, it creates a cycle. Be clear what you will accept and what you won't, and have challenging conversations where you need to. I will come back to this later.

9. Understand how others work

In line with what I talked about earlier, given that people are different, it is really beneficial to understand the working style of those with whom you work closely. This is not to say you need to fit in with them completely, but some acknowledgement is more likely to help you get the results you want. Another simple way is to understand key things about them: their life pattern and, as far as you can, their stresses and strains. A simple example would be understanding that if someone is not a morning person, it would be wise to avoid hitting them with a big issue first thing; if it can wait a couple of hours, that will help enormously. Agreeing how and when you communicate with those around you will enable you to work together.

[5] C. Goyder, *Gravitas: Communicate with Confidence, Influence and Authority* (2014).

> ***Resource 7: Relationship status sheet***
> *Use this sheet to consider your key relationships at work and give them a red, amber or green status according to how positive they are. Then consider why you have given them that status and what you could work on to improve the red and amber ones.*
> **https://gettingonatwork.co.uk/bookresources**

10. Establish positive communication patterns

Regular defined catch-ups are an important part of relationship-building and you need to consider who you should be meeting with and at what frequency. With more remote working happening, agreeing which channels and what frequency is a good tip, particularly for ad hoc questions for which you could normally judge in the office whether someone was busy or not. You can't do this when working virtually. Communication needs to be more intentional in a hybrid or virtual work setting.

Relationships take time, but not only can they greatly enrich your working life but also facilitate and enhance its success. Difficult situations are easier to handle when you have positive and strong working relationships.

How you choose to engage with people is of paramount importance. Considering the method most relevant for the circumstances and what you know about the preferences/situation of the other person/people can greatly improve the effectiveness of the engagement. Some people are happy for you to just call them and check whether they have five minutes to spare, while others prefer an email to arrange something.

Video calls are very useful, particularly when it is helpful to have a visual element and you can't meet in person. However, the phone can be equally good for some conversations, particularly when you already know someone well. It also means both parties focus more on what is being said, as there are no other distractions. Avoid having a blanket way of communicating – give the method some thought. For those with whom you communicate regularly, agree what is best – particularly in a hybrid working environment.

Exercise recap

Resources webpage:
https://gettingonatwork.co.uk/bookresources

- *Trust equation review sheet:* Consider what your strengths and weaknesses are in relation to the trust equation.
- *Gretchen Rubin's Four Tendencies quiz.*
- *Relationship status sheet:* Consider your key relationships at work and give them a red, amber or green status according to how positive they are. Then consider why you have given them that status and what you could work on to improve the red and amber ones.

Points to remember

- Know, like and trust are the foundations of positive professional relationships.
- Trust takes time to build and is multifaceted. However, it greatly facilitates relationships and difficult situations.

- People are different, so you will need to alter your style and approach according to the situation and the person or people involved.
- Understanding different approaches to expectations can lead to more effective self-management and dealing with others.
- Working on the 10 key relationship skills will greatly improve how you relate to others.

Further reflections

1. What prevents you from building stronger relationships?
2. Which of the top relationship skills do you need to focus on?
3. How do you and your team members fit in the *Surrounded by Idiots* and *Four Tendencies* models?
4. How do you need to adjust your behaviour and ways of engaging with different colleagues when they differ from you in these two models?
    a. What do you need to consider specifically when you believe a colleague is mainly in the quadrant diagonally opposite you on the *Surrounded by Idiots* model?
    b. How could you think differently and deal with a colleague who was the opposite to you on the *Four Tendencies* model?

Chapter 7
Internal relationships

Do you know a range of people at work at different levels and in different teams? Most of the time, people focus on the immediate relationships around them in their organisation – the obvious ones, such as their line manager or other people with whom they work most closely on a daily basis. These relationships matter and need time invested in them; however, there are other considerations. Colleagues outside this group can influence both your day-to-day role and your longer-term career. For instance, a big project is unlikely to always get signed off by your immediate boss; often, more senior approval is required. Likewise, when you are being put forward for a promotion, these more senior people are highly likely to be involved in the decision.

The other important point is that we tend to spend most time on relationships with the people we really like or who are 'like us'. It is important to think differently, and to consider objectively who you need to build professional relationships with. Often it will take more effort, but it is likely to pay off tangibly by creating new opportunities.

This chapter is about the internal relationships you need and what to focus on. You need to work with certain people every day – some less frequently and others who may be strategically important for your career path and the clients and/or projects you get to work on. It is important to spend time on all these types of relationships – both the obvious and the less-obvious ones.

What makes a difference to career success

What can make a real step-change in people's careers is getting to know a wider range of people across their organisation. In 1996, Harvey Coleman looked at what drives career success, and termed his findings PIE theory, with PIE standing for performance, image and exposure.[1] The results often initially surprise people, until they reflect on it further. This is because, as Coleman states, 60% of career success is due to exposure – who knows you; 30% to image and just 10% to your performance.

A common initial reaction is that this isn't fair, and it means we need to spend time 'schmoozing' or sucking up to others. However, when you think of the logic of it, people can't know what you do unless they know you exist. You are the centre of your own world; each other person is the centre of theirs. Therefore, often people – especially more senior people – won't know you, as their focus areas and preoccupations are the centre of their own world.

This means you have to be intentional to ensure the 'less obvious' people in your organisation know who you are.

Consider a situation where you are being put forward for promotion by your line manager to more senior people. The first logical thought they will have is 'Do I know this person?' The next thought in their mind is likely to be 'What do I know

---

[1] Harvey Coleman, *Empowering yourself: The organisational game revealed* (1996).

of them? What do I think of them?' In other words, they are considering your image in their mind – what you are like.

Fundamentally, if you are being put forward you must be doing well at your core job; otherwise your line manager would not be speaking up for you. Additionally, in most cases senior people in companies and firms believe they employ good people which is why performance accounts for just 10% according to this theory.

Coleman doesn't go into detail about how the theory applies to career stages, but my view is that his theory holds true for more experienced professionals. However, for people at a junior level, performance will matter more as they need to build their core expertise and reputation. Image is likely to still matter a great deal, and at very junior levels exposure to others is more of a bonus. However, the sooner people start to get into the habit of getting to know colleagues outside of their day-to-day work, the easier it will be! As a middle to senior person in your company, working on your exposure and how you are perceived is of pivotal importance.

There are other benefits to building these more strategic relationships too, apart from it facilitating promotion in the way I have described. Knowing a wide range of people will help you stay up to date with what is going on around your organisation and benefit from a range of perspectives; you can gain knowledge from others and potentially consider other areas of the business you could work with or in. It may also create increased opportunities to collaborate and, where relevant, cross-selling opportunities with clients.

Many service companies and firms don't maximise the opportunities they have for cross-selling. Consider a solicitor who has just done some conveyancing for a client; are they also referring them to their wills and trusts department, as this is often a required complementary service? If not, it is a missed opportunity for the firm. However, this won't happen without strong internal relationships. No solicitor will pass a valued client onto a colleague who they don't know or don't trust, as a negative experience for that client with their colleague could impact their own professional reputation.

One of the main reasons I see for this lack of knowledge of fellow colleagues, and therefore insufficient levels of trust, is that individuals don't typically make the time to build the strategic relationships they need internally. Being able and willing to refer business will not only positively impact your company or firm, but will also help you to build your personal reputation and ultimately your career success.

It isn't just tangible client opportunities that come from people building these less-obvious strategic relationships, but also role opportunities. In this regard, I want to mention my client Pauletta. She had worked in a large financial services company for several years but, despite her line manager encouraging her to go for promotions (in which the line manager herself was a decision-maker), Pauletta didn't succeed. She was continually told 'maybe next time' without receiving any concrete feedback about what she might need to work on to increase her likelihood of success.

We established that this boss was probably playing a game, so I worked with Pauletta to find another way. We looked at the other departments where she could use her skills and abilities, as well as where she already knew some of the senior people. Fortunately, she had already done some strategic relationship-building. We prioritised the relationships for her to focus on, based on the existing relationship strength and the potential role opportunities. We then made a plan for her to work on developing those relationships further.

The specifics of that plan depended on the individual situation, and ranged from increasing awareness of herself and finding out more about the department through to having upfront conversations about forthcoming opportunities. It was really important that we considered the different individuals, their departments and the existing relationship dynamic between Pauletta and each person.

Within a few weeks, Pauletta had been invited to apply for several different roles. The outcome was that she was offered a role a level up that included far more responsibility and people management than her previous one. This example was particularly fast-paced; often positive outcomes take more time, but this demonstrates the value of building broader relationships at work.

Remember, even if you dislike the culture and working environment in the area where you currently work, depending on what you do, it may not mean you need to leave the company or firm altogether. If you can see other departments where you could carve out a suitable next role, then it is worth looking into; culture and ways of working can differ even within one business, and by team.

People always think the next career move is about moving up; however, a lateral move can be beneficial too. Gaining experience in another function or department can be highly valuable in some sectors/professions, so is definitely worth considering.

How to build strategic relationships

The first challenge with building strategic relationships is time. With an already busy job, it can feel like just another thing to do – and it is. However, it needs to be done for the sake of your career, as well as in many cases improving your day-to-day working life. I work with my clients to build a strategic relationships plan, and you could also develop one.

You need to start by putting some time aside to think about why you need to build strategic relationships (objectives). This may include more effective working with other teams, being able to confidently cross-refer clients if that is relevant, building your profile or other factors, depending on your role. The next step is thinking about who would be good to know for each objective (a person who could help you achieve it) then make a plan for (re)connecting with them. You may need to call on others you know already to help you – particularly if you have never encountered the person at all and you only know the job title, not the individual's name.

You are likely to need to prioritise which relationships to focus on so that you can do it well. If building broader relationships isn't something you are used to doing, start with two to three people.

Do this upfront thinking and planning, then allocate regular time in your diary for progressing your plan. Even if it doesn't happen every time it is in your diary, it will happen more frequently than if it wasn't in there at all.

This plan needs to be reviewed every quarter to check it is still valid. For instance, if one of your goals was to find more out about another department to see whether you might want to make a lateral job move and you've done that and decided not to, then you may prioritise other objectives and relationships.

Resource 8: Strategic relationships plan
Use this sheet to consider which 'less obvious' people you need to know.
https://gettingonatwork.co.uk/bookresources

I'm sure you are now concerned about how you connect with people if you don't know them at all. There is, of course, the direct approach. Most of the time, people are willing to help as long as you don't put too much of a burden on them – either with regard to how much time you want from them or what you want from them. Being open about wanting to understand an area of the business in more depth, saying you think there may be collaboration opportunities and/or indicating that you'd like to understand more about their progression are all good possibilities for starting to engage with new people in this way. If you are reticent about this approach, consider your own response to someone making such a request. Most people are happy to help.

The other way is to think about relevant crossovers. For instance, if you have been in a meeting with someone, connecting with them soon after is a good idea – potentially even if they aren't on your plan – if you think they're someone who it would be helpful to know, due to their role or their reputation and the degree of influence in your workplace.

If you work in a large company or firm, another way can be to get involved in something outside of your role. It is a great way to meet people of all levels and from different departments, divisions or practices who you might not usually come across. This could involve joining a committee for an internal networking group or some other area of interest, such as raising money for charity or taking part in a sport. Make sure there is some genuine interest for you in it; it shouldn't just be strategic in terms of meeting people. You won't come across as genuine and engaged if you are not really interested.

The final obvious way to get to know people is to attend any internal networking events that are held, run some of your own or attend external events that your colleagues may also attend (not that it's good to stay with colleagues at an external event – but it can be a talking point and a reason to connect afterwards). Look for opportunities to build strategic internal relationships!

Power can be more than positional

Who you need to know is about who has influence in your workplace. Frequently, people think of power and influence as being about the level of seniority, and this is certainly an important factor. However, there are other types of power and it is worth considering those too – both in terms of your own power and the power that others have. To provide some food for thought, I will explore some of the others here for you.

Sanction power could be about personality, but also could relate to the type of role (not just seniority). Consider compliance as one example. In a bank, if compliance doesn't sign off a new product, then it can't go to market – no matter how much senior people might want it to. The same applies to *information power*, where some people are experts in their area and are required to provide information for projects to progress.

Proxy power is worth considering. Personal assistants often hold this power. They very often facilitate access (or not) to people with whom you may want to meet.

There are more personality-related types of power too, such as *charisma power*, where someone has a strong personal impact and engaging personality so they have naturally become an influencer and gained power – think about Marlon Brando as the Godfather. Likewise, people who are good with *favour power* help others and then ask for favours in return. There are many types of power, so it is worth considering which types you may have that you haven't thought about before, as well as those that others hold.

> ***Resource 9: Types of power sheet***
> *Review this sheet to think about your power sources and which ones you could work on developing. Consider your colleagues and what power they have.*
> **https://gettingonatwork.co.uk/bookresources**

The relationship with your line manager

This is one of the most important internal professional relationships for which you have responsibility. Many think it is the responsibility of the line manager to lead the way, but working on the relationship is a joint responsibility.

With increased seniority, most of the challenges people face are related to other people. There is more discussion of 'office politics' in Chapter 9; however, it is important to acknowledge that most political issues typically occur with senior people who individuals don't directly report to or work with, due to the lack of relationship. Most people, due to the nature of how they work, build a relationship – positive or negative – with the senior person to whom they report or with whom they work most closely.

Building this relationship positively is extremely important and well worth the time investment. This is not only because you need to work with this person frequently, but because of the potential influence on your career – particularly if that person is well respected, liked and therefore influential in your organisation. Consider your future roles but also what you work on day to day and the level of support you get. There are a lot of 'less than good' managers out there; however, building a positive relationship with your manager is more likely to increase understanding between you for more effective and harmonious working, as well as increasing the chances that they will support you in front of others and be proactive in speaking positively about you and your work. Combined with your own exposure-building, this is very powerful.

With your manager, it is important to engage the top relationship skills covered earlier. When you come into a role or you get a new manager, the starting point should be to think about where they are coming from and what their assumptions might be. If you move into a new role and that manager has had an active role in selecting you, it is likely to be an easier start than if they had no say (unusual) or they came in after you or in your absence – for example, when you were on parental leave or on long-term sick leave.

Someone I advised in this area was Gina, an individual who was returning from maternity leave to find herself working for a new manager. She had heard all sorts of feedback from her colleagues, very little of it positive. My advice was to bear it in mind but not to act upon it and assume it was true (as we explored earlier, negative cycles can start based on an untrue assumption).

We discussed a potential dynamic at play relating to Gina being perceived as a threat. She had been at the company for many years, and before her maternity leave she had been promoted and was responsible for many tasks and people in the team. While she was away, she was likely to have been mentioned a great deal. Therefore, the new manager could potentially have built up a certain view of this individual and even felt threatened by her return, as she had been there for some years and clearly knew the department well.

The really important element here was for Gina to return to work and engage effectively with her manager, to listen to her and understand recent happenings, to show willingness for them to work together, to agree how they would work together and, importantly, establish positive patterns of communication. Otherwise, it would be easy for miscommunication to start and for any preconceptions that had been formed to gain traction and impact reality – even if they weren't true.

Considering your manager's perspective and showing empathy for it will go a long way toward building rapport, so in a situation like the one just described, a simple statement such as 'Yes, I've worked here a long time but not for the last year, so it would be good to understand what has been happening and your priorities for the team' could help a great deal. In an instant, it shows respect for the manager and a willingness to listen and engage. This is likely to reduce any defensiveness that a manager may have. It's the same if a new manager comes in while you are in your role. Getting to know them and how they like to work, and helping them without appearing to be a threat, are key behaviours to ease the relationship, as well as being helpful and supporting them as they get to know the organisation.

Building trust and a positive and consistent personal brand with your manager will reduce the likelihood of challenges, as they are more likely to be clear about what they can assume you will get on with and that you will ask when you need their input. Of course, this is a negotiation once you understand how your manager likes to work; some managers want more updates than others. Make sure you agree what works for you both.

It is best to tackle any challenging topics with your manager early on so they don't create further misunderstandings. Some managers may prefer to have discussions as issues arise; others may be happy for you to 'save them up' for a regular catch-up, unless it is urgent. There is no single right way, just the right way for the two of you to engage.

Another aspect you may want to discuss if you manage a team is how the team members engage with your manager. If they are working on their exposure, then they should be engaged with your manager to some degree. However, there needs to be a clear line so that they aren't going over your head.

If you have specific thoughts about your career (which you hopefully do), articulate them to your manager and not just in annual reviews. You can't expect them to just know and you are ultimately responsible for your own career. Some managers will readily support you and other managers may challenge your desired next steps. This can be for positive or negative reasons.

My client Armelle wanted to progress but wasn't sure how to do so, or even into which role. When she discussed with her manager her desire to move forward, he suggested she do some exploratory work and come back with what she found. When she had done this and presented what she wanted to work toward, he didn't seem supportive or encouraging; in fact he was dismissive. It was almost like he hadn't really meant her to do the exploratory work he suggested. She decided to look at options outside her company. When we started working together, we looked at how to revisit this conversation and how to position it for the specific circumstances, as well as rewriting her CV and making sure she had an excellent LinkedIn profile – just in case!

In raising the topic again with her boss, Armelle communicated how important this was to her and demonstrated that she'd reflected further on where she wanted to go next and how she might approach it. She also sought to consider her manager's interests and consider who could step into elements of her role in the team so he wasn't left with a gap. Without manipulating the truth, it is always essential to consider others' circumstances and therefore position what you have to say so it provides answers and reassurance for the situation in which they find themselves.

Following this step, the manager was willing to engage with the potential way forward, so he facilitated some broader conversations within the business. He and my client then worked on a plan regarding the way forward. At the time of writing, my client was making plans to move countries for her new, more senior role. While the breakthrough could have been down to positioning, it equally could have been a test – even a subconscious one – by the manager, to see how much my client wanted to pursue this opportunity and therefore whether she would raise it again and how much thought she would give to it.

There are times when your manager is unwilling or unable to help you get to where you want to go next. Some can't be bothered, while for others it may be a lack of time or they may even feel they aren't well connected or well thought of within the business; it is also possible that they lack the confidence to speak up for you. It is important to think about possible reasons for any lack of support and, where possible, address them with your manager directly. If you still make no headway, then it may mean you need to focus even more on the other strategic relationships you are working on. Very often, those people will then influence your manager and even engage directly with them, which can help you to move forward.

The key messages I have for you here regarding your career development and line manager are to involve your line manager early on in your career thoughts and don't give up too easily: some managers actively put up barriers to see how much you really want something.

Leading and managing others

If you manage others, or expect to do so in the near future, it is common to find yourself in this position without any training or development. I see it regularly. People are promoted as they are great at their core role, but that doesn't necessarily mean they are good at people management – it is a completely different skill set. The exceptions are that some people have innate skills and some adapt to it positively, as they have already informally managed others and/or they have had an excellent role model in a line manager during their career.

Line managing others might feel challenging at first, as it involves a different range of skills and for the most part involves you moving out of the level of detail you were once in (and perhaps really enjoyed!) and delegating.

If you have been managing others for a while but haven't really given it serious thought, now is the time.

Once again, thinking about the key relationship-building skills I covered earlier is key for successful line management. However, there are other considerations beyond that. Considering your personal brand can help you to think about how you want to characterise your leadership style. What would being a 'good manager' mean for you? What would you like people you manage to say about you?

One of the biggest mistakes I see is individuals moving into a people-management role and not making any time to get to know the people they are managing. They then quickly feel the team they are managing is more of a burden than an asset.

When you move into this position, a pivotal task is to understand your direct reports – what they look after, what they are good at, what they are like as people and what their challenges are. Then establish how you can best work together. Individuals often see a new manager as an opportunity for change and improvement, so take this opportunity to listen to what is working well and less well. If they have read this book, then hopefully they are also keen to listen to your vision and thoughts about the team.

I had a client, Annie, in the investment industry who had been promoted from among her peers, which created issues as some of them felt she wasn't the right person for the role. On top of this, the previous team leader had been off sick a great deal during the previous year. She was also particularly friendly with one of the team and there had clearly been passing on of information during that time.

The absence of a team leader for so long meant the whole team had effectively got used to reporting to and engaging directly with their boss's boss on a regular basis. When my client was promoted, these lines had to be redrawn, which involved her establishing her leadership style with the team and setting boundaries. It also involved working with her manager to help uphold these boundaries and send the team to her for relevant discussions and decisions. Her relationship with her boss was pivotal to the success of her leading this team.

She also had to work on the individual relationships with her team. Understanding what drove them, what was concerning them and how they wanted their careers to develop was fundamental so we could work on what action she specifically needed to take. It was a delicate balance between building trust and open dialogue while also establishing a leadership style, team norms and boundaries. Over time, it was a great pleasure to see the situation improve.

Understanding and harnessing people's strengths in the team will make the team more effective and create a more positive environment to work in, but this takes time. Your ultimate goal should be to make sure tasks are being done by the right people; this means delegating appropriately. To promote the growth and development of the team, tasks should always be done by the best-equipped most junior person possible. That way, everyone gets some degree of challenge and uses their time well. If people are spending time on tasks that really could be done by those a level below them, then the potential growth and development of the team won't be achieved. When you delegate, it demonstrates that you trust your team. Of course, there is an element of 'chicken and egg' here. However, often when people feel trusted, they step up to achieve what they need to, asking for help where they need it.

Letting people work on something that is challenging is pivotal to their growth. There are ways of managing this that will depend on the person, but regular check-ins to reassure you both and/or a communicated openness to support that person, as required, work well. Some individuals may need help to get started; others may be better at starting and need some input later on. If you know your team members, you'll be well placed to work out what needs to happen.

Regularly engaging with your team members to make sure they are clear on what they need to achieve and supporting them with challenges, as well as discussing their development, are really important. If individuals feel their careers matter to you and the organisation, they are likely to be more motivated in their day-to-day work, and focused overall. If they haven't thought about building their exposure and network, then prompting them to do so is helpful. Consider also the forums available and the people with whom you can talk about them and their work positively. This will also reflect well on you as a manager.

Your team members need to be crystal clear on what is expected of them, both as a team and as individuals, so you need to have clarity on this, as well as on your management style. Working out how communication happens – especially in a virtual or hybrid working situation – is of pivotal importance. Where you can, stick to what is agreed and avoid cancelling team meetings or one-to-ones unless you really have to. If you regularly do this, it will encourage others to do likewise and/or make the team members feel as if they don't matter to you, creating a sense of disconnection. It might seem a good short-term solution to free up time, but it can cause long-term damage to team morale and performance. If you do need to cancel or postpone, make sure it is not a regular occurrence and a reason is given beyond 'I have a lot to do'.

This switch to managing others is a pivotal time to consider the content of Chapter 5, as line management and people development need time allocated to them.

Likewise, you need to make sure you provide your team with regular feedback. Most companies have a formal process, but feedback needs to be more frequent and informal too. It is hard to talk meaningfully about feedback from six months ago.

Be as clear as you possibly can with any constructive feedback you give. Wherever possible, give examples so the person understands exactly what you mean. I often have clients say something like, 'My manager says I need to improve my presence.' That can be interpreted in many different ways, and varying assumptions made. Do they mean in all scenarios? Do they mean specifically one element such as voice or posture? If you genuinely want to support someone's development, then providing high quality, regular and clear feedback is one of the best actions you can take.

Remember to give positive feedback to the steady members of your team too – the people who do a good job and require less of your attention. Make sure you check in with them, recognise their achievements and challenge them to develop.

Hybrid working can benefit individuals in terms of managing their life and can also assist companies in terms of reduced office costs. However, as a manager you have a responsibility to ensure that hybrid working is effective. This means collating people's views and setting some clear parameters. If this isn't done well then negative 'office politics' could be the outcome as people make wrong assumptions and negative patterns begin. You specifically need to make sure you get enough visibility/time with those you manage. The biggest danger is that you end up rating the team members you see/interact with more regularly more highly. This is less of a risk when people are more consistently in the office.

Remember that you are a role model! You need to manage people well and be approachable so that they have the conversations they need to with you. Losing people results in loss of knowledge and time, not to mention the inconvenience and financial cost of recruiting new staff.

As you can see, there is a lot involved in building positive professional relationships internally, but it is worth taking the time to do it well. The benefits both day to day and in the longer term are many.

Exercise recap

Resources webpage:
https://gettingonatwork.co.uk/bookresources

- *Strategic relationships plan:* Use this sheet to consider which 'less obvious' people you need to know.
- *Types of power sheet:* Review this sheet to think about your power sources and which ones you could work on developing. Consider your colleagues and what power they have.

Points to remember

- Building relationships beyond the 'obvious' people internally can dramatically impact your day-to-day working and career success.
- People need to be aware of you and have an impression of you to get to know your work. Good performance alone is insufficient for career success.
- There are different types of power beyond positional power, so it is worth considering these.
- It is vital to invest time in building a relationship with your line manager.
- Equally, if you lead and manage others, commit to getting to know those people and supporting their development.

Further reflections

1. How could you improve your exposure at work? Reflect on who else needs to know you and how you could start.
2. Consider your attitude to 'office politics' and how you might be perceived because of your behaviour in ways that perhaps you don't intend.
3. How strong are your work relationships? Consider what you need to work on with your line manager and the people you manage.
4. Watch and assess the power dynamics and influencing techniques in a situation that is new to you – for example, attending a council or school meeting.

Chapter 8

Building external relationships

Who knows you outside of your organisation? If you are in a client-facing role, there is probably a reasonable list of people. However, you do need to think beyond your current clients, keep prospects in mind and consider those who may be key referrers of new clients. Of course, if you aren't in a client-facing role, it is easy to think that you don't need to work on external relationships – I will come back to this later on, as this isn't the case.

While relationships have always played an important role in winning new business, in times gone by newspaper ads and the phone directory would have been important too. Today, people can consult a range of sources in seconds – LinkedIn, online reviews and their personal network – so you need to consider how you use those opportunities. There is more to do to maintain your reputation and your relationships. This chapter will look at why external relationships matter and how to build your external network over time.

Good client management

The relationship skills covered in Chapter 6 are extremely important when dealing with clients. They need to feel valued and that you genuinely want to provide them with excellent service. If you build trust and a great relationship, they are less likely to move away even if fees/prices increase. They will rationalise that it isn't worth the hassle, a view that will be reinforced by the loyalty they feel toward you personally.

The additional benefit is that happy clients will mention you to others so you get warm referrals – a much easier way to build your client base.

Making time to build client relationships and engaging with them is vital. Getting to know how a client likes to be serviced and communicated with impacts what the relationship is like; being proactive and anticipating a client's needs makes all the difference. Some clients may want regular updates; others require them only when there is a challenge or point to discuss. Some may prefer to speak on the phone, others to communicate by email. Take the time to get to know their preferences and how best to support them.

You need to make sure your clients have a positive experience no matter how or with whom they interact at your company or firm. If you manage others who interact with your clients, it is imperative that there is clarity on how you work with them, including the roles and responsibilities.

It is helpful to build client relationships at different levels. If you rely on one person and they leave, your work is in danger. This can be an opportunity for your team to engage at different levels.

Things may change in how you service clients, including systems, fees and processes. Guiding your clients through these will help smooth the way. Anticipating their challenges and putting yourself in their shoes will help a great deal. There is a key reason why businesses lose clients: they make changes that work for the business but either don't work for the clients or aren't well handled – the business fails to think about it from the client's perspective.

If you inherited your clients and haven't yet brought in new ones, this is a priority. Retaining clients is the easiest way to keep the numbers up, but for growth and to offset client attrition that may happen for reasons unrelated to you personally, you will need to attract new ones.

You might think this section on client management is shorter than you expect; however, there are many sections in this book that apply to your client relationships if they are a part of your working life. There are various 'touchpoints' mentioned – such as in-person meetings, phone calls, video meetings, your online profile and email communication. You need to think about how you come across and engage with your clients via each of those to provide them with a high-quality, consistent experience.

Resource 10: Client relationships template
Use this document to consider your key client relationships, their strength and what you could do to improve them.
https://gettingonatwork.co.uk/bookresources

You can't build a network the minute you need one – that is, when you need a new role or to start developing new business – so the sooner in your career you build the skills and confidence regarding networking, the better, even if it seems that business development responsibilities are not in your remit at this point in time. It's not just about building relationships with direct clients, but also with potential referrers. It's a long game, but being top of people's mind when someone, or their friend or colleague, needs what you offer is key.

Networking beyond business development

I see it all the time: many people in large organisations under-estimate the value of networking and they realise too late how helpful it could have been.

Of course, if you are responsible for business development, then being able to network well is vital; new potential clients are, of course, important – but so are existing clients. Seeing clients at events that aren't meetings about everyday matters is an important way to further build the relationship.

You may be thinking at this point that you don't need to network as your role is not a client-facing one and/or you will never have responsibility for business development. This is a major career mistake that people commonly make.

There are plenty of other reasons to network beyond business development, including:

1. *Staying current in your sector or industry.* It is beneficial to go to conferences, to hear what is happening and speak to peers in other organisations. It can help you think about what you might want to do differently at work or what to consider that you hadn't before.
2. *Getting yourself known in the market.* Much of the job market is now 'hidden', and many people with strong networks find their next role via their network. You may be 100% happy in your role now, but you don't know what the future holds so a strong professional network will provide you with more options.

One of my contacts, Fiona, had always moved jobs due to a previous boss moving on – a boss who valued her and who would eventually ask her to join their new organisation. This was a real positive, as it showed that her previous bosses had valued her work, skills and abilities. She had delivered great work and had certainly worked hard to build her reputation with her colleagues. However, she had become complacent about her career path and eventually 'office politics' conspired against her. Her career expectations were dashed at the company where she was working with a previous boss, and she needed to leave.

Unfortunately, she realised she had no external network despite being relatively senior, which made her job search particularly challenging. It might not seem 'the right way' but you'd be surprised how many roles not only get filled via networks but also get created for specific people.

3. Another reason to get to know others outside your organisation is if you have a role where you need to *find suitable suppliers or partners* to work with.

A helpful way to think about networking is as 'building mutual beneficial relationships'; 'selling' should not be your key association with it.

Your networking strategy and plan

Very few people love networking, but with the right plan and skills, you can enjoy it more and get more from it.

If you are new to attending networking events, try a few different ones. There are many types: conferences, informal drinks events, lunches and specific group meetings. Some may have a formal element where you need to speak about yourself briefly to all attendees, while others don't. The easiest are those where networking is not the main focus, such as a conference. This not only means the majority of the time is about listening to speakers, but also that it is easy to find topics of conversation when you come to the networking part.

Thinking about your impact the moment you are at the event venue is essential; we've all spotted someone from a distance and come to the judgemental conclusion that we hope not to get stuck with them! You don't want to be that person.

Naturally, your sector and awareness of the type of event you are attending (think formal lunch versus relaxed evening drinks event) are important to consider in planning appropriate dress and behaviours. You need to think about your personal impact and brand: you are representing yourself and the organisation for which you work. Refer to Part 1 of this book to consider this.

When thinking about your networking strategy, two key elements matter: defining who you want to meet and considering where you are most likely to come across them.

If you have a good network already, there is the very direct route of asking people you already know to introduce you to specific other people. LinkedIn is a good way to see who knows who – there will be more on this valuable tool in Chapter 10. At the other extreme, having an eye out for ongoing opportunities is a great mindset to have if you generally get introduced to new people as part of your role.

However, many people need to be more intentional. Essentially, this means attending events to meet others. Once you know who you want to meet, you can find events that are most likely to attract those people. The great benefit in time is that, once you get to know people, you will hear about other events that are often unpublicised and by invitation only.

Resource 11: Networking strategy and planning sheet
Use this sheet to consider how networking could benefit you, who you might want to meet and how you could find out about relevant events.
https://gettingonatwork.co.uk/bookresources

Key skills for attending a networking event

Getting to a networking event a little early or on time can make it easier, especially if you are slightly anxious. This is because there are less likely to be groups formed already, so it's simpler to get talking to others and potentially the host too, who may then introduce you to others. Another good tip is to head to the coffee stand or bar to get a drink immediately as that is often a great opportunity to get chatting to others in a more relaxed way.

However, if this isn't possible or it hasn't resulted in a conversation, you will need to find someone to talk to. It is best to decide where you are heading before you reach the middle of the room; otherwise you will end up bobbing around in a sea of people and this won't help your confidence. While some people will actively invite you to join their group, others will not, leaving you stranded.

When looking for a group to join, look for 'open' groups where there is an easy space for you to slot into. For example, avoid joining the pair who are standing exactly opposite one another in an intent conversation, as this will be awkward. Choosing a group with an uneven number of people can often work well, as the conversation is rarely balanced between them all. Avoid a large group unless there is a clear gap and/or you know someone in it well and know they will be pleased to see you.

It might sound odd, but it can be good to approach someone who is on their own at the side of the room, often leaning up against the wall. Even if they are on their phone, it is probably their comfort blanket as those who have something important to attend to are more likely to leave the room to sort it out. Yes, the conversation might be awkward as the person may be shy, but they are also likely to be grateful that you approached them.

Reconnecting with people you know, as well as new people, is essential. Relationships take time to build and it is only by seeing people over and over again that rapport and trust are more likely to be established, so it's not always about increasing the number of people you know. I have a large network but I don't like and trust everyone I know. I might like someone but it doesn't necessarily mean I'd refer them to a client of mine. For some of these relationships, this may change as the relationships become more established.

When joining people, it can be good to utter 'May I join you?' – although if joining a conversing pair or group, you can slot into the gap and wait for a pause in the conversation to greet people. One of my concerns is the conversation turning to be completely about me, so I usually introduce myself by name and then invite them to carry on their conversation and I will join in as and when it seems appropriate.

The reality is that people will always be conversing, so you just have to join and integrate. At this point, a smile and good eye contact go a long way toward building rapport. Repeating your first name twice with a pause in between can be a good way to make sure someone takes it in, as odd as it sounds: 'Hello, I'm Joanna, Joanna Gaudoin.' This is particularly important if it is an in-person event with no name badges, as it can reinforce your name and avoid the other person forgetting it and feeling embarrassed. If you forget a name, it is best to be upfront and ask again, or wait until they introduce themselves to someone else. Repeating someone's name after you first hear it can help you retain it more firmly in your memory.

In terms of conversation, I would suggest that there are four key stages. As mentioned earlier, the first stage should ideally never be about what someone does. This is limiting, as it makes it challenging to go back to everyday conversation. If you consider someone asking, 'What do you do?' as the first question, it can feel like a vetting procedure. It can make people feel like the response needs to meet some criteria or else they will go and find someone else to speak to. Some people do so for this reason, but others just don't know what else to say.

Start with points of commonality – what they thought of the speakers if at a conference, where they travelled from, whether they have attended this event before, how they heard about the event. It might sound cheesy but it is important to be human first, as we looked at earlier in relation to colleagues. Listen for what people mention that you can pick up on and ask about.

The next stage is asking about their professional life. Doing this first helps them feel valued; it is more polite than just going straight into talking about yourself and it helps you learn more about them to angle how you phrase what you say about yourself. Remember that at this stage listening is vital in order to continue to build rapport. If you spot a top opportunity at this point, then note it in your mind but avoid jumping in; it is better to link to it when you come to speak.

Speaking about what you do should be the natural next stage. What you say will depend on who the person is. For instance, you are likely to explain what you do in a very different way to someone in your industry versus someone who isn't part of it. You want to make your explanation as engaging as possible. Stating a job title rarely achieves this. The best way to think about it is to consider what problems you help solve, for who and in which situations – this could be in relation to external clients or internal ones. Considering a few options for expressing this in advance can be extremely helpful.

The final stage is really about what happens next, so if in the conversation you have agreed on discussing something further, then it's about confirming that you will contact them to arrange that conversation; alternatively, it might simply be agreeing that it would be good to get to know one another more in a general way.

At the very least, it should be connecting on LinkedIn. I often ask people whether they are on it and, if the answer is yes, I say I will send them an invitation.

Making a follow-up commitment will keep it more firmly in their mind so they won't be surprised when you get in touch and it will also make you more likely to do it as you've reaffirmed what is next. This is often a good point at which to exchange business cards if you have them, so you have one another's details. Even in this increasingly digital world, I think they are still useful – especially when following up the next day. You can get your phone out and make notes or use an app while you are with someone, but I believe it creates a barrier.

Once you have agreed what is next, you then need to leave the conversation. A good tip is to leave on a high, not when you have exhausted all conversation avenues. This can feel strange, but it also means you have a reason to meet again, and renew and continue to build the relationship. Leaving a group is easy: affirm how you have enjoyed meeting the people and say you are going to talk to a certain person across the room or to meet some other people.

Avoid leaving someone on their own at a networking event. If you have ended up with the shy person by the wall, ask whether they'd like to go and get another drink (you might both encounter new people to talk to) or say you should both meet some other people and integrate into another group that has a gap for the two of you. Other options include changing your body language to encourage others to join you or, if you are sure the other person will be happy, introducing them to someone else you know so you can, in time, get into other conversations. Leaving them alone to 'go to the bathroom' will undo any rapport you have built, and even if they are not someone you intend to stay in touch with, doing this can negate any other positive outcomes, such as them introducing you to others they know who could be useful contacts. There is always another option rather than 'dumping' them!

At an event, you don't want to just meet a couple of people, but likewise you don't want to be seen as one of those eager people trying to tick off as many contacts as possible, so consider the balance of quantity and quality regarding interactions.

What to do after a networking event

Afterwards, follow up on all you need to as soon as possible. If you don't do this, you have wasted a lot of time. There is nothing worse than the person who is all enthusiastic at the time but who then doesn't do what they said they would (remember reliability in the trust equation). It negatively impacts your reputation in a serious way. This means you need to be careful what you commit to at the event. I find this is particularly important in terms of who else you might introduce someone to. In the moment, it can seem a great idea to connect them to your client but in the cold light of day this may be less the case. If I think there is a really good reason to connect a new contact to someone else, I always give the caveat that I am going to check with the other person first; otherwise, you can create a very awkward situation.

In terms of who to follow up with, I suggest that if you like the person and you think there are some potential opportunities even if they are not obvious at this point (for example, you work in the same or related sectors) – then that person is worth staying in touch with and building the relationship further.

Networking in the long term

Consistency is needed, as sadly people will quickly forget you, so you need to have a strategy and a plan. Plan to go to regular events that suit you. If you are not a morning person, don't commit to breakfast meetings. Consider what is realistic for you. It is better to commit to fewer events and actually attend them. Over time, you probably want a mix of opportunities to meet new people and reconnect with others on a regular basis.

Having specific people in mind to stay in regular contact with is important too. I use my diary, but you may wish to create a spreadsheet or task list, or use your organisation's CRM system. These continued interactions could range from email check-ins through to regular coffees or lunches. It is only over time that you will realise the value of your network. Knowing people helps you get introduced to others and come across more and better opportunities, both in terms of your current job role and for the future.

LinkedIn can act as an address book for those you meet at networking, so making these connections after the event is essential (always with a message). The search capability is such that, even if you forget someone's name, you can generally find them using other criteria if you are connected. LinkedIn is also a great way to feel you have seen someone more recently than you actually have if you see their posts. This can make reconnecting even many months later easier, as you can refer to what you have seen there. Events themselves are like the planting of seeds; work is needed over time to get those seeds (the relationships) to grow. Building a diverse network is valuable – you never know how it will generate and support future opportunities.

A word on virtual networking

The Covid-19 pandemic meant we weren't allowed to attend events in person. Off the back of this, many virtual events sprang up. The time-saving benefits of these meant some people who struggled to get to in-person events, predominantly for personal reasons, could attend. It also meant the world opened up further and it was just as easy to network with someone across the globe as it was with someone in your own local area.

The downside of networking online is that it is harder to build rapport – particularly because you often can't freely select who to have one-to-one conversations with. It is easier to avoid being led astray by initial perceptions and potentially have conversations with those you wouldn't have spoken to in person; however, the opportunity for genuine conversations is far more limited.

My message would be that if virtual networking is the only way you can realistically network, or, if the key people you need to build relationships with are abroad, then make it part of your working life. However, if you can go to in-person events instead, I would highly recommend that you plan to do so.

It is easy to become so busy in your day job that you never consider who you need to know externally, whether now or in the future. I couldn't encourage you more strongly to make time to get to know your clients, and to build your external network. It does get easier with practice.

Exercise recap

Resources webpage:
https://gettingonatwork.co.uk/bookresources

- *Client relationships template:* Use this document to consider your key client relationships, their strength and what you could do to improve them.

- *Networking strategy and planning sheet:* Use this sheet to consider how networking could benefit you, who you might want to meet and how you could find out about relevant events.

Points to remember

- Whether you have internal or external clients, make the time to get to know them well.
- External networking is a valuable activity even if you don't have business development responsibilities.
- Develop a networking strategy and plan, and work on the key skills to network confidently and effectively.
- Have a process and system in place for building and nurturing relationships over time, even when you are very busy.
- You can't build a network the minute you need one.

Further reflections

1. How good are you at client management? Remember that clients can be internal.
2. If relevant, do you tend to retain clients and get referrals?
3. What currently prevents you from networking or, if you are networking, what do you think you could do better to achieve an improved outcome in terms of building a good network?
4. Consider how you can build relationships better over the longer term. Are there some people in your network with whom you want to refresh your relationship?

Chapter 9

Common people challenges

As I discussed earlier, issues with other people are responsible for the majority of challenges you will face at work. Not thinking about others' perspectives, getting into negative patterns with people and/or not understanding the role you have played in a situation are among the biggest reasons why these issues occur.

Different cultural backgrounds can, of course, play a part, as culture has a big impact in terms of how people see the world. However, I believe that all too often it is easy to blame cultural differences and make them an excuse for not working on individual relationships and dealing with challenges.

The groan of 'office politics'

The mention of 'office politics' usually provokes a negative reaction. Often, people think of words such as gossip, back-stabbing, sucking up and cliques in association with this term. It is often linked to some people having more power than others – sometimes beyond their role, as discussed in Chapter 7.

When 'office politics' is negative, there is a negative environment at work – productivity and morale are low and decision-making takes more time. This is often because people don't want to say what they really think or share information.

It can cause individuals to experience a lot of stress, be off sick from work and ultimately leave.

It is a fact of life that where you have different people with different values, beliefs and assumptions, there will be politics. What makes complete sense to you won't necessarily make sense to others because they aren't coming from your standpoint and are likely to have differing values, beliefs and assumptions.

However, 'office politics' doesn't always have to be negative. The danger is that negative cycles can start unless people consider 'office politics' and their own role in it. Frequently, as an individual, you are likely to think everyone else is political – but how do they see you? We all have a role to play.

You can see how it happens. Imagine you have a colleague who speaks up easily and frequently at work – sometimes too frequently, in your view. This seems even more the case when an influential senior person is around.

In one particular meeting, that person takes the floor to speak on a particular topic, which normally would be covered by your joint line manager. In your mind, this is perhaps inappropriate and showy. However, unbeknown to you, your line manager has asked that person to do the presentation but just didn't let you know and nobody signposted this in the meeting. This solidifies your previous view of the person, who indeed is confident to speak their mind most of the time. From now on, you are wary of this person, feeling they are always trying to look better than you – even though this may not be their objective at all. However, this can affect how you behave toward them, which they then react to. This is an example of how negative cycles start.

Very often, it isn't just the person you are reacting to but your own feelings and situation. Take a scenario where you approach the coffee machine at work and two of your colleagues, a man and a woman, stop talking. Why is this?

If you think about it, you can probably come up with four or five reasons: they were talking about you; they were having a confidential conversation; they are having an affair(!); their conversation came to an end; they were being polite so they could include you. In that instant, you won't think of all of those reasons; you will think only of one – which may or may not be true. If that morning you had a heated discussion with one of the people or you simply got out of bed grumpy, you are more likely to think of one of the negative reasons. Can you see the danger of these situations?

It is hard in the moment to think objectively, and you must be savvy about what is going on around you; however, it is essential to avoid jumping to conclusions. Being as transparent as you can be in your communication will help others be the same in theirs. You can't change others' behaviour except by changing your own.

You need to consider how others could perceive your actions without knowing the context. Consider a catch-up with your opposite-sex boss over lunch in a restaurant. Some people may deliberately try to spread misinformation about this. In this example, ways to avoid creating a void where people fill in gaps include being very transparent to others about whatever is happening, such as mentioning it in conversation or being very obvious when you leave for the lunch.

Think about the conversations you have had with individuals in advance of a meeting where you are presenting a proposal. You wanted to get their thoughts on how to position your proposal or what exactly it should look like. Others might say that was political; you'd probably say it was sensible!

When I ask people in group sessions who they have most political issues with at work, the winners are always peers and senior people who aren't their boss. Peers makes complete sense, as often there is a natural feeling of competition – particularly as there are usually fewer roles at the next level up. One short piece of advice is not to focus wholly on points of comparison between yourself and your peers. Instead, consider what your strengths are and which of your skills and capabilities you need to build on based on your own perceptions and feedback. Focusing on others in a comparative way is rarely helpful. Instead, consider how you can best work together to leverage one another's strengths.

More senior people usually come out as a political headache because individuals haven't built these (strategic) relationships, so when they come to something where the senior person's input or approval is needed, those people are likely to be more reticent, which can be seen as negatively political – another great reason to build those strategic relationships. To have more support at a broader level among senior people will pay off both in your daily work and career wise.

People often question how to stand out to senior people – my two pieces of advice here would be to focus on building individual relationships and to take opportunities when they come up – there is more on this in Chapter 7.

Shifting 'office politics' to a positive focus starts with individuals and happens team by team, so don't feel defeated. Before you give up on your role due to negative politics, try changing your behaviour for a while and see what happens.

Opting out of 'office politics' is not an option if you want to progress your career; as we saw with exposure-raising, doing a good job alone is sadly insufficient. You need to learn how to navigate different situations.

Halting negative 'office politics'

My big message related to 'office politics' is to consider how you are being perceived – how do your actions and behaviour look from the perspectives of others? For instance, if you give one message to one person and a different one to another, it could get you into difficulties. Knowing what is being said in the office is useful, but being seen as a gossip is not, as nobody will trust you when it comes to important information. Ultimately, to navigate 'office politics' positively, you need to communicate clearly and build your networks. There will always be those who behave badly to get what they want, but it's rarely good practice if you want to feel positive about your working life.

The only two ways to stop negative cycles in their tracks are to question new information and the beliefs and/or assumptions you hold, and to change your behaviour.

One of my clients, Alison, had a dynamic with one of her team that whenever she asked him to do something, he would challenge and question her. Of course, this questioning can be important but the issue is that it loses its effect if it is a continual behaviour and it can be very annoying for the person making the request to seemingly have their judgement questioned all the time – even for simple requests. 'Just get on with it' or 'because I say so' are rarely the best responses in this situation, as they will make the person resentful and defensive. My client was frustrated with it and silently groaned a lot.

We looked at Gretchen Rubin's *Four Tendencies* (covered in Chapter 6) and established what her profile was; we also discussed her team member's potential profile. From this exercise, she realised that by simply explaining more of the 'why' when making a request, he was more likely to get on with it without challenging her every time. To be clear, the motivation wasn't about justifying her request each time, it was about optimising the chance of him valuing the task and doing it. This very simple change has been one factor that has led to a now much more positive relationship, where there is now greater mutual respect.

As mentioned, you can't change others' behaviour except by changing your own. Think about a relationship that is challenging and consider how you could start to behave differently in your interactions with this person – both proactively and reactively – then see what happens. It's about breaking cycles! Letting go of the past is important in this process.

Another tip is to think about how you can position something so it appears advantageous to the other person. Very often, there are some all-round benefits; it's all about positioning. It might sound clichéd, but wherever possible you want to look for the win–win situation. Of course, making your request with empathy will also help, so something like, 'I realise you have been working hard on x and this makes it more challenging but could we discuss how we could deliver it a week earlier?' This will go down much better than a blunt request.

It isn't always possible, but where you can, think about how doing something in a different way or to a different deadline would benefit not only you but also the wider team, as well as the person of whom you are making the request (it needs to be credible). Consider wanting to move the deadline forward on a project because your boss is clamouring to see something earlier. This is probably going to put the other person under increased strain and they may not much care that your boss would like to see it earlier. Thinking about how you can get what you want in a way that would benefit them is key before you make your request. This could be related to additional resources to get it done sooner or enabling the person to move on to something else they want to focus on earlier.

With some people, you may need to explain the rationale behind a decision or action. If you can't reveal more about why you are asking them to do something – for example, related to a confidential matter – then explain this up front and say you will update them as soon as possible.

Dealing with difficult situations

Very few people would say they enjoy conflict. Conflict is also a word with negative connotations. Many people have a tendency to avoid challenging situations and conversations. While carefully choosing what we raise is important, constantly avoiding the conversations we need to have is a negative behaviour and is likely to lead to greater difficulties further down the road.

Difficult situations are really defined by what you consider difficult and awkward to raise, but could include a variety of situations. This ranges from bringing up a performance issue with someone in your team to offering a differing view in a meeting, or explaining to someone that the way they spoke to you was not acceptable. It may be task based or behaviour based, or both.

Difficult conversations usually involve issues or people we care about, so feelings are often involved. When issues aren't dealt with or you don't feel heard, resentment frequently builds, and negative patterns can start once again. Likewise, avoiding a challenging person at work is rarely a good idea, particularly if working more closely would be beneficial.

You are not bringing your full value to work if you don't share your opinions and views, even if they differ from those of the majority. Sharing them may also help someone else be more up-front and encourage deeper conversation and discussion in a meeting to potentially achieve a better outcome. Even if an outcome is the same as it would have been if you hadn't shared your viewpoint, it can often make people more sure that the agreed way forward is the right course of action.

The Thomas-Kilmann model (Figure 9.1) is helpful for considering your attitude to difficult situations.

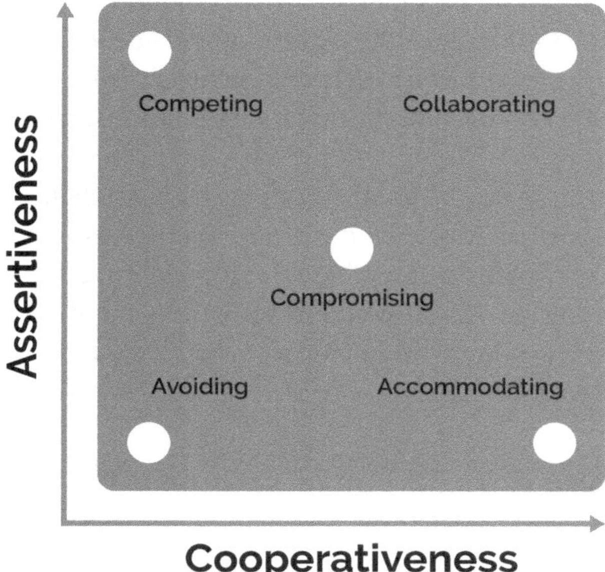

Figure 9.1 The Thomas-Kilmann instrument

Original figure is available at www.kilmanndiagnostics.com/overview-thomas-kilmann-conflict-mode-instrument-tki

Once you identify where you typically sit in the grid, you can consider the situations in which you may want to consider engaging differently. The model states that there are different times to operate in the different quadrants. For instance, if you are the most senior person available in a crisis and a quick decision needs to be made, you will want to assert yourself and move forward with your view (top left).

However, if you are not the most knowledgeable in a situation, then while it is important to begin the discussion, you may cooperate with someone who is more knowledgeable on the topic (bottom right). The bottom left quadrant is really only the place to be if there is a lot of emotion involved and it would be best to raise the issue another time, or if the situation is likely to be a one-off event that won't cause resentment to build up or any other future issues if it is not raised.

Compromise can be good, but this isn't possible in all situations – particularly when it is a case of one action or another with no in-between possible. The top right quadrant is the one to engage with if you and the others involved have an equal level of knowledge and so need to work on the challenge together.

Tackling difficult conversations

The first point to keep in mind is that difficult conversations are important to have. From there, there are some key elements to consider:

1. Establish how the other person or people involved have made you feel and consider whether that was really the intention

Take the scenario of your boss dismissing your request for a pay rise when you know others in the department are paid more than you for the same type of work. That is likely to leave you feeling under-valued, frustrated, annoyed and unfairly dealt with. Unless you have had feedback that you need to dramatically improve your performance, that is probably not what your boss intended. It is important to consider why your boss didn't grant it. There could be any number of reasons (reasonable or otherwise), but you won't know why unless you go back to them and have another conversation. In that conversation, it is important to show empathy (a common theme here), thereby potentially acknowledging that there are cost pressures or that it was an 'out of the blue' request before saying that you'd like to discuss further and understand more about why they declined your request.

By initiating a conversation at a later date, it shows you have considered the situation carefully and it is therefore less likely to be seen as an emotional reaction.

It is also important to consider whether what someone has done or said challenges you personally. Let's take a situation where you have been given some constructive feedback that you lack attention to detail – something you believe you excel at. Hearing that is going to be very hard – far more challenging than feedback on an area you don't believe you are strong in. Sometimes that can cloud your ability to see what the other person could be seeing, so it is important to be aware of this.

2. Make proper time for difficult conversations

This is essential. You need to do justice to the difficult conversation so it is far better to arrange a meeting to discuss the situation properly rather than tacking it onto or hijacking another meeting, as that won't help you achieve the best outcome.

3. Consider your role in a difficult situation

Thinking about any of your behaviours or actions that could have contributed to where things are now will help you approach the conversation with greater humility. It will also lessen the opportunity for any surprises in what the other person or people may come back with that are linked to you and your behaviour.

4. Avoid blame attribution

Avoid either lumping all the blame for the situation on yourself or the opposite – assuming you had no role to play. The reality is usually somewhere in between.

5. Listening is a key skill in this situation

Making sure both of you feel heard in the situation will help you to move forward together to work on resolving the issue. If someone doesn't feel heard and acknowledged, then you won't be able to move forward. Paraphrasing and checking your understanding are great tools at this point to make sure you have clarity and to ensure the other person feels valued.

6. Avoid dressing up bad news

Of course, in a performance review situation, you are likely to be giving both positive and constructive feedback; however, in other situations don't try to sweeten things; it is better to be up-front about what you wish to discuss in factual language while showing empathy and acknowledging your own feelings. Presenting your opinion or view as absolute truth is definitely something to avoid – not just in words, but in terms of tone and body language too.

7. Extrapolating a situation to make a judgement

For instance, if you think someone's action is selfish, it is rarely helpful to say so as that is what they will react to, rather than the issue itself. A very useful phrase is, 'How would you feel in my situation/from my perspective?' (having explained your situation and/or assumptions).

8. Staying calm is of pivotal importance

Otherwise the other person is likely to be responding to your emotional state, rather than the facts of the situation. When you are unhappy with a situation, it is easy to get carried away, so focus on the key areas that need discussing rather than expressing all your frustrations related to that person or situation.

9. Check any assumptions you have

This is a good habit to get into, as otherwise it can skew the conversation if the other person has completely different assumptions. Remember that assumptions come from your knowledge base and the specific situation you find yourself in. What makes complete sense to you may not do so to someone else. As one of my clients said, 'It depends how many feet someone is flying at as the view can differ significantly at different levels.' Even with a lot of listening, it can sometimes be difficult to fully understand someone's position and resulting behaviour, but you need to try!

10. Being open to being persuaded

This is an important attitude to have in mind if you are truly going to problem-solve with the other person. It is also worth asking them what might persuade them to have a different view or position. Being open and a little vulnerable is most likely to help you reach a good outcome as it will encourage the other person to be open too.

Taking an initial step in these conversations is hard, but with time, your relationships will improve if you tackle what needs to be discussed. As we saw previously, the more effort you put into building these relationships at the start, the easier these challenging conversations will be.

Considering how you interact

Considering again the patterns we get into with people, it is worth thinking about the manner of our exchanges and the mode you are in. Eric Berne's transaction analysis[1] concept is very useful.

It is worth reading up more on this theory if you aren't aware of it. Essentially, it says we transact with others in one of three ego states: adult, parent or child. Clearly, in your professional life you want to be engaging with others in the adult state; however, I have frequently had clients who have had other states coming into play. Take the manager with a team member who is always late delivering work. The temptation is to go into parent mode, telling them they must do it on time and what will happen if they don't.

This could also be done in an adult way with the right tone and language. However, if it isn't, you risk the person reacting as a child, which is going to start a very negative pattern of interaction. Equally, a transaction can start with the team member approaching you in a child ego state, which could push you into a parent ego state. It is a continual challenge to keep interactions on an adult-to-adult basis for the most productive outcomes and the most effective and positive relationships. After all, who likes to be engaged with on a parental or child level at work? It can happen very easily, though. To be in an adult state, consider your tone and

[1] E. Berne, 'Intuition v. the ego image', *The Psychiatric Quarterly*, 31, 611–627 (1957).

body language. Also, asking rather than telling will help, so it is worth inquiring why work is always late and how you can support the person to avoid it happening again. Simply telling them not to deliver late is unlikely to have a good outcome.

The power of vulnerability

As mentioned earlier, saying you don't know can be hard. I have found this to be the case particularly with bright people with in-depth knowledge and expertise in a given field. Of course, you don't want to tell clients or colleagues you don't know all the time; however, being able to do so when appropriate is very powerful. It makes you more credible when you do know. Also, as long as you commit to finding out in a given timeframe and sticking to that, it's an opportunity to build trust and credibility. People will appreciate that you value their question enough to spend time finding the answer. It is unrealistic to expect you to know the answer to every question you are asked; likewise, it is important to admit when you have been wrong or have made an error – people will respect you far more. It also gives them less reason to question you at other times to establish if you are covering up a mistake or hiding something, as you are known for being up-front.

Frequently, people don't ask for help when they need it. Being aware of your strengths and weaknesses is important in relation to your day-to-day work and also in relation to others. Involving others when something is not your strength and you need input is a must if you want to build positive professional relationships. Others will feel valued, you will come across as genuine and credible, and you will gain knowledge

– as opposed to pretending to know things you don't. You can't know everything!

If you have a suggestion about which you are unsure, or that you think is obvious or could have already been considered, the simple starter phrase, 'You may have considered this, but...' can be very helpful.

When you disagree

You may experience what you perceive to be over-confidence from a colleague and you may disagree with what they are saying. All too frequently, people bowl in too quickly with their objections and the flaws they see in what is being said. Considering how you can do this in another way so you are less likely to get a defensive reaction is an important skill to master. Listening fully, even if you think you know what someone is going to say, is important. Simple questioning about how the person foresees their idea working in different scenarios is a powerful way to explore whether it really is a good idea and is far less likely to get their back up. 'How might that work in x scenario?' said with a look of puzzlement and in a curious tone will encourage them to show you that they have thought the idea through, enlighten you and change your view, or get them to realise that they have more work to do.

The right level of detail

One of the biggest challenges I see among my clients is getting the level of detail right – both in terms of what level of detail they should be involved in for their role (and what they need to delegate) and, even more importantly, the detail they share with others – particularly more senior people.

Getting to know others' preferences is one aspect – some bosses will want to know the detail, others just the headlines. It is also likely to depend on the topic.

One reason why people often don't get promoted is that senior people fear a level of detail will be lost once you have moved on from that role. It is essential to consider whether you think you are too far into the detail and share too much. It also makes it hard to be perceived as someone who is ready to step up if you are bogged down in it. People will not only draw the conclusion that it would be a challenge to lose you from the current role, but also that you are less capable of seeing the big picture – a vital skill at more senior levels.

Always consider carefully what your audience really needs to know. Also have in mind who really needs to be involved. Particularly in virtual meetings, having too many people involved dramatically impacts effectiveness.

Succession planning

A final word on why people sometimes don't get promoted is that there is nobody suitable to fill their place, so if you are looking to be promoted or make a lateral move, consider who you are preparing to potentially step into your role. It will help to have a culture in your team of encouraging people to step up and stretching them. If you manage others, then this is a key objective. It also keeps people engaged and motivated.

Resource 12: Key people challenges assessment
Use this document to consider what your key people challenges are and how you can approach improving them.
https://gettingonatwork.co.uk/bookresources

Being heard

Many people don't feel heard at work. This can be particularly challenging in larger meetings, especially on the phone or in a video call.

In a face-to-face meeting, you can use your body language to indicate that you want to speak – for example, moving forward in your chair and using hand gestures. These are important skills to work on (although some people will be oblivious or choose to ignore them, if they wish to).

Tone of voice is another way to command attention – speak at a steady pace and a loud enough volume, without hesitation.

To build on what I said earlier, working on key relationships as well as your personal impact and brand will help you a great deal. Then your input is more likely to be sought. For some meetings, you may want to have some advance conversations to discuss relevant input that you want to contribute.

People challenges can feel exhausting, so if that is where you are now, tackle them one at a time or one relationship at a time. Consider what behavioural changes you could make to positively impact the situation in which you find yourself. Keep the key relationship principles from Chapter 6 in mind too.

Exercise recap

Resources webpage:
https://gettingonatwork.co.uk/bookresources

- *Key people challenges assessment:* Use this document to consider what your key people challenges are and how you can approach improving them.

Points to remember

- You can't opt out of 'office politics' if you want to progress your career.
- It is easy to think others are political, but it is vital to consider how they perceive you. Actions and decisions implicitly make sense to those carrying them out, but not necessarily to other people.
- You can't change others' behaviour except by changing your own.
- Avoiding difficult conversations and situations is likely to lead to longer-term challenges.
- Seeing situations from another's perspective and listening will facilitate positive conversations and problem-solving.
- The level of detail you are involved in and share is important to consider.

Further reflections

1. How do you deal with conflict and challenging situations? Is this holding you back? How could you change your approach?
2. Consider what negative patterns you are in with different people and which behavioural actions you could take to encourage change and break these patterns.
3. What behaviours and ways of interacting could be holding you back from progressing?

Part 3

Professional scenarios

You have considered your own impact on others and why and how to build and navigate professional relationships, including common challenges that may arise. Now is the time to consider more specifically the different professional scenarios where people encounter you and how to master those scenarios to achieve what you need to do, optimise your relationship-building and ultimately enhance your career success.

At this point, I would encourage you to take some time to think about the obvious relationships around you at work and who else you need to know (building on what was covered in Part 2). From there, you can think about where you encounter those you have a professional relationship with (I call these 'touchpoints') – the obvious and the less obvious – to help you consider what to work on. The chapters in this final section can then act as a sense check for these and give you specific guidance on what to consider in these scenarios.

Resource 13: 'Touchpoints' review sheet
Use this sheet to help you to consider the 'touchpoints' where you encounter others and which you need to work on most.
https://gettingonatwork.co.uk/bookresources

Chapter 10
Online presence

It's obvious to consider the impact you have on others when you are interacting with them directly. Even if you hadn't thought about it before reading this book, you should now have a good idea of why and how you have a positive impact on others, particularly in your professional life.

What people often forget, though, is the impact they have through less obvious means when their presence is 'passive' – for example, online.

The internet generally

The internet is full of all sorts of information and often people are surprised what it tells the world about them. If you have never done it, it is worth bringing up a private or incognito web browser window and searching your name to check what is freely available online about you. It is particularly important to review whether there are any photos of you online and whether you want them to be visible to professional contacts. Check you are happy with what is there and that it doesn't contradict your personal brand and the perception you want to create. That is an easy start.

If you are on social media, then reviewing your settings is a sensible thing to do, to make sure any personal photos and comments are only viewed by friends. I have a policy of not being 'friends' on social media with people I know professionally, to make sure there is a clear line. This might seem a harsh boundary to have; however, someone who is a peer and even a friend at work now could use what they see against you, share personal information about you with others at work or one day even be your senior – or you could be theirs – and you might not want them to have access to information on your whole life. Once access is granted, it is often hard to remove without the reason being obvious.

If necessary, you may need to make it clear on social media profiles that comments are yours and unrelated to your organisation – although the reality is that an organisation is represented and communicated about by its people, so care and caution are needed.

Why LinkedIn matters

In most professions, a good LinkedIn profile is now an expectation rather than a 'nice to have'. Since the increase in remote working, LinkedIn is used far more even by internal colleagues to look others up who they are due to encounter. This is because they haven't met them casually around the office or heard anything about them from others, due to reduced office working. Professional contacts will often think it strange if they can't find you on there. It is not only relevant when you want a new role – indeed, it will serve you poorly in this regard if you only see it that way, as it takes time to gain traction with a profile.

LinkedIn is an opportunity to build your personal brand further and reinforce your credibility. It gives you the chance to build your brand with a wider range of people who you know and don't know, far beyond what you could achieve by only meeting people in obvious professional settings.

You want LinkedIn to have a push-and-pull effect, so your profile is there for people who have heard of you elsewhere but equally for new people to come across you. Even if you are not keen on social media overall, I would strongly suggest you are present on LinkedIn. If you are concerned about privacy, there are lots of settings you can put in place regarding access to your information and it's not about sharing personal information: the focus is your professional life.

Your LinkedIn profile

If you haven't built much of a profile until now, it is worth allocating two to three hours to work on it. If you do that well, then a check every few months should be sufficient to update it with anything new. It shouldn't just be about job changes.

LinkedIn helpfully gives you a grading as to how complete your profile is. Additionally, to prove it is worth the effort, note the data associated with your profile, such as the number of profile views, before you make any changes. You can then review how this data improves over time when your profile is more complete and showcases your skills and experiences more meaningfully, as well as when you've been more active on the platform.

Before you make any updates, change the settings so that every change isn't visible to your network. You may want to change this back just before you make the final change so that your network is encouraged to view your profile.

You want to optimise your profile for two key reasons. The first is so it looks good and people are encouraged to read it and feel it reinforces the person they know, if they know you in real life.

The second is so it appears in searches; this is pivotal if and when you are looking for a new role and if you have responsibility for business development. The key contributors to showing up in searches are you being active on the platform (which I will come to shortly), having over 500 connections (at the time of writing, this is still apparently an important factor in you showing up, due to the algorithm) and having a fairly complete profile that takes into account key words that are relevant for who you are and what you want to be found for.

Like networking, even if you don't have business development responsibility, LinkedIn is still highly valuable.

The following are the key areas on which I get clients to focus:

1. *A photo that looks like you now.* This is so people can find you quickly if they have met you before, especially if you have a common name. When meeting someone new, you never want someone spending half the meeting working out what is different from your LinkedIn photo. This photo needs to be appropriate for your job role and represent your personal brand positively.
2. *A banner image at the top, so your profile looks like you bother about it.* This can be something related to the area in which you work or the geography, or even something more personal (with care). Check that it works well on the app version of the platform too.
3. *Headline – a job title can be dull and mean little outside your organisation.* Consider whether you can put more about what you do in an interesting way – for example, rather than 'family law solicitor', try 'helping families resolve their disputes quickly and

conclusively'. You might want to include key words such as 'solicitor', but it doesn't always need to be in such an obvious way.

4. *'About' section.* This is the opportunity to say a bit more about yourself: what you have achieved, what you enjoy, what your expertise is and how you help those you serve – whether internal or external clients. Exactly what you include will depend on what you do and the main objective of your LinkedIn profile. This is an important section for keywords.
5. *Experience section – this should not be a download of your CV nor should it only be job titles.* Add some information so people can read about your main responsibilities and what you have achieved in each role. Make sure all titles and timelines align with your CV if you are looking for a new role.
6. *Education – consider what is relevant to include.* If you have been working for 20 years and have a degree, then it isn't relevant to include school qualifications. There are additional sections you can add for courses, awards and so on, so consider where you want different elements to feature.
7. *Skills – this is a good way to showcase what you are good at and, again, to influence searches.* You may or may not get endorsed for them by others, but that feature doesn't carry a lot of weight so there is no need to focus on endorsements.
8. *Recommendations – these are valuable.* This is an opportunity for people to understand more about what you are skilled at and what it's like to work with you, from those who have actually done so. If you are client-facing, it is highly valuable to get some from clients (always ask offline first); colleagues' recommendations are important too, including from more

senior people, peers and those who have worked for you. You may need to give people a structure to follow for their recommendation to increase the chance of them completing it – such as why/in what situation you worked together, what you did, what you were like to work with and the outcome.

9. *Additional elements.* You can add many different sections, so if you have been a volunteer or contributed to publications, consider what you want to feature and where it best sits. You don't have to get too personal, but LinkedIn does give you an opportunity to show some of your personality and build your brand.

If you complete these sections well, you will be on your way to a great profile.

Resource 14: LinkedIn profile checklist
Use this checklist to help you complete the relevant sections of your LinkedIn profile.
https://gettingonatwork.co.uk/bookresources

Building your visibility on LinkedIn

I mentioned that you want to see LinkedIn as push and pull. In terms of contacts you have met elsewhere or had for a long time, it is a great way to remain visible to them (this doesn't mean you shouldn't have a clear plan for staying in touch with key people in other ways!), assuming you and they are active on LinkedIn.

A good way to see LinkedIn is as your professional contacts address book. The search function is very helpful, so even if you can't remember someone's name but can remember some things about them, such as company and location, you can find them. This only works if you are diligent about connecting with others – which means connecting with everyone you meet in real life, whether in person or virtually, such as at meetings or at a networking event.

If I am introduced to someone by email, I often wait until I have had a more meaningful connection with the new person before inviting them. Always write a message, too; it looks very lazy not to, even if you have only just met them. The only exception is if you are literally inviting them to connect while speaking to them and they know you are doing so.

When you set up your profile, invite people you know professionally, as well as appropriate personal contacts.

LinkedIn is highly valuable for enabling 'new' people to find you. They may find you from a search anyway, but the more active you are on LinkedIn, the more your profile is likely to show up. You don't have to spend hours crafting content: a few minutes of each day for engagement is plenty. The LinkedIn app is extremely helpful for this, as you can easily use it while waiting for the kettle to boil or the train to arrive.

The easiest way to explain the interaction options is as a hierarchy of activities:

- *Interacting with others' posts* with one of the emotion buttons – always make sure you read the post fully first!
- *Commenting* – this is a great way to show engagement and knowledge, or to share an opinion you may have. This action can help those outside your

immediate network to become aware of you. For instance, the connections of the person whose post you commented on may see your comment, particularly if they have also engaged with the post.
- *Sharing* – when something is useful or interesting for your network, you can share it. Always add a comment to introduce what you are sharing and potentially explain why. You can also send posts to specific contacts via a message.
- *Creating your own content* – this could be a post, a post with a poll or even an article, for example.
- *Searching for relevant contacts and connections* – as long as you aren't pushy, you may be surprised by how open most people are to connecting. Again, always include a message.

LinkedIn regularly updates the platform, so stay on top of these to keep your profile and visibility up to date.

Who you accept connection requests from is ultimately your choice. I tend to accept anyone from industries that are in some way related to my work. If they haven't sent a message, I send them one asking what prompted them to connect with me. I am often positively surprised by the response, and this can start an interesting conversation.

At the time of writing, I have had an issue with just one person in a decade and ultimately you can disconnect from them and/or block them so there really is no problem with connecting. I even connect with 'competitors' if they invite me. I don't wish to sound arrogant, but people who want to work with me do; those who want to work with someone else are welcome to pick the person who best meets their needs and with whom there is personal chemistry. If you are client facing, this is worth thinking about.

The degree to which you interact on LinkedIn will depend on what your aim is, but no matter what your situation, plan to be visible regularly! Otherwise, it is obvious when you are job hunting, and by not using the platform effectively you are likely to miss out on the opportunities offered by LinkedIn.

Resource 15: LinkedIn visibility sheet
Use this document to plan what activity you will do on LinkedIn.
https://gettingonatwork.co.uk/bookresources

Exercise recap

Resources webpage:
https://gettingonatwork.co.uk/bookresources

- *LinkedIn profile checklist:* Use this to help you complete the relevant sections of your LinkedIn profile.
- *LinkedIn visibility sheet*: Use this document to plan what activity you will do on LinkedIn.

Points to remember

- Make sure you are aware of what the internet says about you.
- Develop a positive and informative LinkedIn profile.

- Seek to engage with others regularly on LinkedIn. It keeps you in their mind even if you haven't seen or spoken to them for a long time.

Further reflections

1. Where do you need to audit your online presence?
2. What opportunities could you create or improve from focusing on LinkedIn?

Chapter 11

Meetings and presentations

In the everyday work environment, we interact a great deal with others. You probably see most of these interactions as part of the day job. However, it is important to consider how you could maximise opportunities to improve the way you are perceived and to improve your relationship with others. Two key interfaces are meetings and presentations.

Meetings, meetings

We all spend a high percentage of our working lives in meetings. It is important to consider how effective they are.

On average, employees spend almost 23 days a year in meetings, with 13 of these days being unproductive, according to a recent survey of European workers conducted by Crowne Plaza Hotels.[1] In 2017 research done by the *Harvard Business Review*, 71% of 182 senior managers said meetings were generally unproductive and inefficient.[2]

---

[1] L. Brown, 'Employees waste nearly 13 days a year in "unproductive" meetings, survey finds', *People Management*, 21 September, www.peoplemanagement.co.uk/article/1742498/employees-waste-13-days-year-unproductive-meetings-survey.

[2] L.A. Perlow, C.N. Hadley and E. Eun, 'Stop the meeting madness', *Harvard Business Review*, July–August 2017, https://hbr.org/2017/07/stop-the-meeting-madness.

What is your experience? Do most meetings drain you, or do you come away energised because you've collaborated with others and got stuff done? Many of my clients feel the former emotion. Not only are ineffective meetings draining, but they also use up valuable time and can lead to people working longer hours than necessary as they end up doing their 'actual' work in the evening or at the weekend.

The main issues I see my clients experience with meetings seem to be around lack of participant engagement, poor time-keeping and lack of meeting follow-up.

Attending meetings

You may feel you don't have much control over the meetings you attend. However, I would argue that, even as a participant, you have a role to play in shaping the effectiveness of meetings – you shouldn't ever be a passive bystander.

Everyone attending a meeting should be clear on what the aim of the meeting is. Is it an update? Is it to generate ideas? Is it to work on a problem? Is it to make a key decision? Is it to inform? At a more granular level, what is the specific desired outcome?

Without this clarity, you will struggle to have a productive meeting and achieve the desired result. If you are a participant, it is fine to ask about the purpose of the meeting when you are invited, if it is unclear. It can also be helpful to make sure it is clarified at the start of the meeting, so everyone is aligned and focused on the desired outcome.

You may run out of time in a meeting and you might need to book a follow-up, but it is more likely to be focused if everyone is clear about the purpose, desired outcome and their role in it. If it is your meeting, you have an even greater responsibility to establish this clarity. If you do this, then people are likely to be more motivated to attend the meetings to which you invite them and to contribute more fully on an ongoing basis.

If a meeting is going off track, it can be helpful to point this out. Even if this is happening due to a senior person, it is helpful to do this to check everyone is agreed this is a relevant deviation in that specific meeting. It is much better than it just happening, going unacknowledged and becoming an acceptable habit. You want to avoid negative precedents being established. Of course, think carefully about the words and tone you use to do this.

One of the biggest reasons why meetings are ineffective is the attendee list. 'Meeting bloat' occurs for several reasons: people being added over time, a fear of people feeling excluded, a lack of discipline to consider who really needs to attend and a very natural feeling of wanting to include others.

However, when there are too many people in a meeting – particularly in an online meeting – attention lapses. It is easy for people to feel they aren't required, that they can hide behind others and that there is no point trying to speak up unless they are leading the meeting or a key part of it.

As a participant, it is essential to understand why you are attending a meeting (your role) and to be clear what you are expected to contribute, if anything. Are you there to be informed, to be part of a decision, to provide information? As well as being useful to you, if people get into the habit of doing this, then those organising meetings are pushed to think more clearly about who is there to avoid 'meeting bloat'.

Speaking up in a meeting

If you are a quieter person and struggle to speak up, keep in mind what you are there for and that you are valuable. Not being sufficiently visible can hamper career progression. You may want to plan for likely contributions you want to make until you are more in the habit of speaking up. A word of caution here, though: you will never be able to plan for every eventuality, so you also need to be flexible about what may come up and not look like a rabbit in headlights. Remember the power of 'don't know' that I mentioned earlier. Some people's fear of this prevents them speaking up, in case they get asked questions about what they have said; lessen the fear by seeing the opportunities of admitting you 'don't know' – that should increase the impact you can have in a meeting.

You don't want to end up speaking simply for the sake of saying something, so consider what you can contribute that is valuable.

Use your body language to demonstrate that you wish to speak: move forward, lean in and gesticulate. If it looks like a point is coming to an end and moving on, and you still have something to say, then it is acceptable to interrupt with something like, 'Can I add, before we move on…?"

If someone interrupts you mid-flow, say you'd like to finish and carry on – this is important to draw the right boundaries. People shouldn't get used to speaking over you; 'Teach people how to treat you,' gravitas expert Caroline Goyder has said.[3] If you get into the habit of referring back to people when they have tried to interrupt you, that shows respect the other way and people will be less likely to interrupt you in the future.

Avoid repeating someone's contribution to claim it as your own at all costs – this never looks good. A useful tool can be to say, 'To build on xxx' and then add your idea to make it clear you are acknowledging the other person's input but have more to say on the matter; this shows you are not trying to take credit for their point.

Running a meeting

If it is your meeting, consider carefully who needs to be there and make sure they know why – this might involve asking them to prepare something specific for the meeting.

If you have the right people at the meeting, then the next challenge is to make sure everyone can contribute as required. If it is your meeting, it is essential to keep an eye on this. In most meeting settings, there are some who are more willing to speak up than others; watch the body language of quieter people and/or ask for their input directly, if appropriate.

Support others who struggle to be heard or who lack confidence by inviting them to speak if you believe they want to contribute. This is particularly important for members of your team, both to grow their confidence and improve their contributions.

---

[3] C. Goyder, *Gravitas: Communicate with confidence, influence and authority* (2014).

Every meeting should end with a clear idea of what needs to happen next and by when the next steps should be completed; as the meeting chair, you are in a prime position to make sure this is clear and that there is the best possible chance that the actions will happen. If there are lots of different action points for a variety of people, these need to be clear and it is even better to send a brief email to summarise this. If you aren't going to do this, then ask someone else to do so – consider carefully who you ask and how, or invite people to volunteer.

Additional positive meeting behaviours

Where you sit in a meeting, particularly where there are relatively few people, can be key to the ambience that is created. For instance, if you go to meet a client with a colleague, sitting directly opposite the client can create a sense of confrontation and a 'them and us' feeling. This may happen initially – for instance, at a pitch meeting – but with time this is rarely conducive to relationship-building. You don't always get a choice of where to sit, but when you do, consider it carefully. At an informal meeting with one other person, I always try and sit at a 90 degree angle to them.

Meetings can be a great way to build your visibility with more senior people, and to build a perception of you and your personal brand, so it is worth considering how you want and need to come across. It may be worth re-reading Part 1 of this book with this in mind.

Over time, it is good to think about which other meetings may be useful for you to attend and to speak to your line manager about this. Likewise, if you manage others, think about opportunities for them to step up and gain more exposure and experience.

Virtual meetings

Virtual meetings present additional challenges: body language plays less of a role, as you can't see as much of everyone. It can also be harder to speak up; I'm not suggesting you wilfully interrupt others, but the challenges with internet connections mean you can more easily be forgiven for interrupting.

Wearing something colourful that stands out can help a great deal in a virtual meeting. Make sure your background isn't distracting and that you occupy around 50% of the screen area. You neither want to be a dot in the middle or be all head on the screen. If you can make sure your shoulders are in shot and, where possible, hand gestures are seen, that will improve how you come across.

Resource 16: Meeting behaviours review sheet
Download this sheet to consider what you might need to work on regarding meetings.
https://gettingonatwork.co.uk/bookresources

Presenting

What is your attitude to presenting? Being willing and able to present engagingly and confidently is one of the best skills you can develop for your career. This makes you visible and gets you known.

Presenting can, of course, take many forms – from presenting information in a low-key way from your seat in a meeting through to presenting on a stage at a conference.

Those who are unwilling to work on this area are very likely to miss out on opportunities.

Many people feel afraid. Some fear can be good – it gets the adrenaline going and is likely to contribute to a better outcome; however, paralysing fear that causes sleep loss and leads you to stumble over your words isn't.

Many factors contribute to fear, but a big one is people believing that they don't have anything valuable to say and that they will make a mistake. It is important to remember that audiences don't want you to fail. Think about when you watched someone present who was clearly dreading it and was very nervous: you felt awkward for them. People want you to do well and most of the time they want to hear what you have to say, as it might be useful, helpful or even necessary to them.

Remember that although what you are presenting may feel like 'old knowledge' to you, for the most part it is 'new' to the audience, so value it and speak slowly and clearly in accordance with the discussion in Chapter 4, and engage positive body language as discussed in Chapter 3. Wherever possible, you want to take your audience on a journey with you; storytelling is a powerful way to get engagement and to help the audience remember what you said.

If you are reading this and are not used to presenting, then start to take opportunities as soon as you can to present information – even if it is just for a short period of time, perhaps as part of a client report. Even if you're more senior, look for opportunities that you can take to present. Consider what you could present that could benefit you and your company or firm: start small and work up; consider internal and external options. Some people find it easier presenting to new people rather than colleagues.

I had a client named Jeanette who was an accountancy firm partner. She had been a partner for a while but had never really had to present. However, upon joining a new firm she was expected to present to the rest of the firm to update colleagues on the rules and regulations governing her area and to deliver marketing presentations about the firm at networking events. We started with her doing a mock presentation for me so we could understand which aspects of her skills and style were positive and which needed development. We also worked through her fears of presenting. Working on both these aspects over time, including opportunities to practise, enabled us to really focus and give her the confidence and skills she needed to present engagingly and build the required relationships. After all, if she isn't confident with her colleagues, they are less likely to entrust her with their clients and cross-selling opportunities might be lost, as we looked at previously.

There is plenty of material available on presenting well, so I have outlined my top tips below:

1. Think carefully about your audience

This includes who they are, what the purpose of the material being shared is and therefore how to position what you are saying and what the key messages should be. If you aren't clear on what you want to communicate, the audience won't be either. Your job is to take the audience on a journey with you in whatever you are presenting. Fundamentally, if the audience doesn't know, feel, think or act differently as a result of what you share then you haven't achieved your goal.

2. Supporting materials

Creating and using a slide deck can be a valuable tool, but is not relevant in every scenario and if it is, your presentation shouldn't work without you! It is pointless to put everything you wish to communicate on the slides. I think slides can be helpful as different people learn and retain information in different ways, and seeing elements written down or as diagrams/images can help. You need to be the focus, though. If you are using slides, be careful not to talk to the screen. Yes, the slides can be a prompt for what you wish to say but your audience will switch off if you are talking to the screen and not to them.

3. Notes and scripts

Unless you are presenting an extremely formal speech at a lectern, scripts are a no-no. It is better to be less than word perfect and engage your audience than deliver a perfect script with everyone disengaged. You should know what you wish to say (not memorised word for word, either) in terms of the key messages. At most, you could have some prompt cards with single words on them to remind you. If you are using PowerPoint, then your slides should be the prompt. You need to know your stuff yet not be so rigid that anything surprising throws you.

4. Body language

This is pivotal for communicating confidence, engaging others and enforcing your own confidence. Own your space, look at the audience and be deliberate with your hand gestures. Having a clicker in one hand can help a lot if you are standing to present PowerPoint slides! There is almost always one very smiley, reassuring person in the audience. Locate that person early on and, when you are doubting yourself, look at them – making sure you don't end up staring!

> ***Resource 17: Presentation skills sheet***
> *Download this sheet to consider what you might need to work on regarding presenting.*
> **https://gettingonatwork.co.uk/bookresources**

Great presentations don't just happen: they take planning and thought. How you deliver is at least as important as what you present. If you don't keep people engaged, they won't take the message on board anyway! The more you present, the easier it will become and the better you will get at it, so think about how you can improve from where you are at now.

Exercise recap

Resources webpage:
https://gettingonatwork.co.uk/bookresources

- *Meeting behaviours review sheet:* Download this sheet to consider what you might need to work on regarding meetings.
- *Presentation skills sheet:* Download this sheet to consider what you might need to work on regarding presenting.

Points to remember

- Consider how you can make the meetings you lead more effective in terms of who attends, objectives and how meetings are run.
- As a meeting participant, be clear on why you are attending specific meetings and what the expectation is.
- Consider when you need to speak up more frequently in a meeting and how you can do so.
- Presenting information well is a key skill to develop in many organisations if you want to progress your career.

Further reflections

1. How could you improve the meetings you are part of and have a greater impact?
2. Where are you at with presenting? How could you benefit from enhancing your skills?

Chapter 12

Day-to-day communication

How you are perceived is not just about the big occasions – the meeting with your boss's boss, the key presentation. The perception of you and your professional relationships are built each day, even by very small actions.

Considering how you communicate with others, including both the method and the words you use, is fundamental. I'm sure you have dashed off an email that you've regretted later (as we all have!) or hastily called a colleague in a panic.

You can't be perfect, but the majority of the time you need to be extremely considered in how you communicate, to improve the outcome and perception others have of you; this will also mean others forgive the odd occasion when you do slip up.

This chapter will look at the everyday communication opportunities you have with others and how to maximise them in terms of how you are perceived and how you build relationships.

Emails represent you on the screen

We all get many emails a day. How you deal with them is the first important point. Some like to file them as they deal with them; others have literally thousands in their inbox yet still seem on top of managing them; others don't stay on top of them at all.

It doesn't really matter what you do with them as long as you respond to all that you need to in the right way and in the appropriate timeframe.

Even if you are someone who is pretty efficient with their emails, there are times when it is a good idea to wait a little while before responding. This may be to offer a more thoroughly thought-through response, to reduce the number of emails generated by waiting a while and/or not making it look like you have little else to do. Consider who the email is from, the perception you want to create and what you need to achieve with the reply.

You need to set emails out well to maximise the chance of getting a response. Nobody likes to receive an email and see a solid block of text. Consider the layout carefully – use spacing and bullets as much as possible, especially if it is long. This will reduce the 'groan' factor when someone receives it. This groan factor will be even less or non-existent if someone has a positive perception of you (more generally) that is ignited the minute they see your name in their inbox.

Make it crystal clear what you want from the person or people to whom the email is addressed. If it is a long email, you might want to put this at the start and at the end, so if someone just reads the beginning and the action required of them is quick, then they are more likely to reply sooner rather than leave it. An email may be for information only, requesting information or needing sign-off – make this clear.

Think about the language carefully – who you are sending it to and how formal or not you need to be. If it is a new person, avoid shortening their name unless they have done so in an email to you or said to call them something other than their full first name.

Be aware of whether some phrases could be misinterpreted without the recipient being able to hear your tone of voice. Saying key sentences out loud may help you.

If the email is to someone who you communicate with regularly, then remembering something they mentioned to you recently – such as going on holiday – can be helpful to refer to when starting a new email dialogue. Emails are relationship-building opportunities, as well as a way to inform people and get things done.

Consider carefully who is included in an email, as copying in too many people can mean you get little outcome from it as people think they can hide behind others. Avoid always copying additional people 'just in case', as this can lead to negative 'office politics'. It isn't good to be perceived as someone who is always looking to cover their back. Avoid 'bcc' too. If you really want someone to see it who can't be put in the cc field, then forward it onto them separately with a covering note.

Resource 18: Effective emails sheet
Use this document to think about how you can be more effective with email.
https://gettingonatwork.co.uk/bookresources

The power of a phone call

The loss of body language on the phone means you are entirely reliant on your voice and language to communicate. However, phone calls are still an important and useful way to engage with others in addition to all the other technology we have.

They are a step up from an email and a very good option, particularly if you are not sure what someone thinks about a topic and want to find this out. A phone call can be more exploratory than an email. A lot of the time, people rely too heavily on emails and I'd strongly encourage you to consider when a phone call could be more effective. If you know the person, consider whether they are someone who would prefer a call to an email and whether this will be more effective in eliciting a response.

Very often you will learn more from a call – a person's tone and the words they use are excellent clues, which are largely lost or ambiguous in an email; people are likely to give more away during a call than they would 'put in writing'.

Some phone calls you may need and want to schedule with the other person; other calls can be made speculatively. In the case of the latter, it is always helpful once past introducing yourself (assuming the other person doesn't have your number saved in their phone) to check it is a good time for the person to talk – making clear how much of their time you require and for what.

Always consider the tone with which you start a phone call – for instance, whether you sound hesitant or confident, optimistic or negative – as it is likely to set the tone for the call.

Think about what you want to achieve from making the call. If you know the person, think about who they are and the type of relationship you have with them to adjust what you say and how, in terms of tone and language. If you don't know them, consider what perception you want to create.

As with emails, phone calls are great relationship-building opportunities so once again, remembering something about someone you already know and asking them about it – a recent holiday, their unwell mother or training for a marathon – is helpful. It can help to find a picture of the person, for example on LinkedIn, in order to engage more fully with them when you can't see them.

If you are calling someone 'cold', who doesn't know you, then it can help to acknowledge that first off; there is nothing worse than someone that doesn't know you being super friendly on the phone – it doesn't feel genuine. With these 'cold' calls, it is even more important to get the person's attention through your tone and the clarity of what you say. Mumbling your name in a hurried way, for instance, won't help you make a positive impact and command the other person's attention.

As we mentioned earlier, people always think that building their profile and reputation is about the big occasions, the important presentation, the proposal meeting or the client pitch. Yes, of course these are of pivotal importance; hopefully, though, you can see that it is also the seemingly more mundane and common interactions with others that build your profile and impact how you are perceived – particularly with the colleagues and/or clients with whom you work most.

Casual conversations

Even if you are a more task-focused person, as discussed in Chapter 6, it is important to make time for casual conversations with colleagues. Naturally this is easier and more natural in person. Take the opportunity to greet people (I know it sounds basic, but many don't) and talk to people as you see them in the corridor or at the coffee machine. Not only do these short encounters build relationships, but they also help you to build your profile with others and learn more about what is happening and others' perceptions. Arriving a bit early for a meeting or not rushing off immediately at the end are helpful behaviours.

When working virtually, communication needs to be more intentional. If you are entirely home based, then you will need to 'plan' for some connecting conversations to make sure you are building the relationships you need. If you are hybrid working, then be prepared to spend some of your office time having more casual conversations, which might have implications for how you plan and manage your time.

Make time to consider how you can make the best use of your daily interactions to build your personal brand and your relationships, and how you can gain knowledge to help you work more effectively on a day-to-day basis and optimise your career opportunities.

Exercise recap

Resources webpage:
https://gettingonatwork.co.uk/bookresources

- *Effective emails sheet:* Use this document to think about how you can be more effective with email.

Points to remember

- Consider the small daily opportunities you have to build the perception of who you are and develop relationships.
- Spend time thinking about the format of an email to increase the chance of you getting a reply.
- The phone is now often under-used. Consider when this might be the most relevant way to communicate.
- Make time for casual conversations with colleagues to build relationships and gain information and knowledge.

Further reflections

1. How could you improve your emails to get an improved response rate and quality?
2. When could you make calls rather than send emails and how could you use them to build relationships?
3. Consider how you could have more casual conversations and what benefit there might be for you.

Chapter 13

Changing roles

In my experience, the biggest reason why people don't change roles is that they are ill-prepared to do so. As said earlier, for internal roles this usually relates to not training others so more senior people fear moving you up and out of your role as you hold a lot of knowledge. There is also the danger that you haven't thought about how you are perceived and you are not perceived in the right way to make the step up, and therefore need to work to get past that; you need to consider this carefully, particularly in terms of delegating, what you are involved with and the level of detail at which you currently operate, and therefore what others associate you with.

The other reasons lie in not having built the right strategic relationships internally, not having voiced where you see your career going and/or not working on the gaps you need to close to get promoted. With sufficient time put into these areas, internal promotion is far more likely to happen – assuming there are opportunities available.

In terms of external opportunities, good ones can come up when you least expect them, and when you don't necessarily want to move to a different organisation! However, it's not good if the reason why you don't apply for an interesting opportunity is because you don't have time to get the application materials together.

This is why I recommend that you have an excellent CV and LinkedIn profile prepared, which you update regularly. When these are done in a hurry either for a good opportunity you have heard about or because you are suddenly in an unexpected situation, they are rarely going to be of the highest quality and are unlikely to showcase your skills and experience in the best way. This chapter is all about helping you consider what you need to have prepared in case you need or want to go for a new opportunity.

Your CV

Like it or not, the CV is still a very important part of most role applications. Whether a recruiter or company is seeking you out or you are proactively contacting them, a CV is likely to be required.

This is your opportunity to showcase your key experience, skills and expertise, so think carefully about what has a right to be there. Your CV should begin with a summary of you that highlights your key abilities – both technical and people related. This is the part of the CV that is most likely to need tailoring if you are applying for slightly different roles.

You then have the remainder of the two sides (yes you read that correctly, two sides) to highlight your key responsibilities and importantly your achievements. Wherever you can, use data and specifics to provide evidence.

You should also include your education from your degree (if you have one) onwards. Only those in the early stages of their career should include their key school exam results. A short section on any languages you speak and interests is a good way to finish.

Importantly, the CV should be appealing and easy to read. Cramming lots in with no space won't achieve this, so you need to be very disciplined about what is included. This is why I 'reinvent' my clients' CVs; this means I get them to tell me about their roles and it is my job to translate this into a powerful CV to showcase their experience and expertise. What is said in conversation often represents what they enjoy most and what they are best at – very different from when they type up their recollection of their role and what they think they 'should' include.

Ultimately, your CV should serve as a hook to get people interested in you and want to invite you to an interview. Therefore, it needs to tell a clear story of your career with selected highlights covered.

It's obvious, but it needs to be 100% correct in terms of spelling and grammar. It is always worth getting someone else to read it for you, as it is hard to see a document afresh when you have worked on it for so long.

For some roles, artificial intelligence may be used to screen CVs, so it is particularly important that key words are considered carefully. Likewise, you will also want to consider key words used in a job description and how you can include them where relevant.

Resource 19: CV checklist

Use this document to help you assess the strength of your current CV.

https://gettingonatwork.co.uk/bookresources

Make sure you end up with a CV that you believe represents you well and you are proud to send to relevant people. The next step is to consider what people see of you on LinkedIn, which can be referred to at any time without your knowledge.

Using your LinkedIn profile to get a new role

Chapter 10 covered what makes a good LinkedIn profile, so it's worth reviewing this information if you are considering looking for a new role. It can be helpful to use elements from your CV against your job roles, although it should not be a direct copy and paste of everything.

Remember that LinkedIn should serve to be a good reinforcement of who you are to those who have met you elsewhere or seen your CV. It should also help new people to find you. In the case of a job search, this may be recruiters and potentially individuals who work for companies for which you may be interested in working. This is why it is valuable to have a quality LinkedIn profile set up and to have built your network and visibility when you are not even considering looking for a new role. A profile can be set up quickly, but it takes a while to build your network and visibility, and therefore for LinkedIn to surface your profile in relevant searches.

There is a setting that alerts recruiters, but importantly not others, that you are looking for a new role, so you may want to put that on when you are actively looking for a new position.

Your job search strategy

Depending on where you are with your thinking and the speed with which you want change to happen, you may choose to consider your job search strategy before you work on your CV if you are looking for a bigger role change; otherwise, doing it once you have completed your CV is fine.

The first part of this is to consider what you really want in your next role and what are the 'nice to haves'. This should include practical considerations such as flexible working arrangements and amount of travel, through to role responsibilities, including people management. The culture and values of your next organisation are also an important consideration. Doing this exercise early on will help you to make clear decisions about which roles to apply for and, when you get offers, which one to accept, as you can reference your list. It doesn't mean you can't go against the list, but it will help you think more clearly and weigh things up more thoroughly.

You may have several different options you are considering. One client of mine, Peter, was considering five different avenues – a role similar to his previous one and four other options.

I worked with him to create an excellent CV and LinkedIn profile to showcase his skills and experience. We also established how to get the information he needed to evaluate the different career route options and then to distil that information and discern his approach to the market. This resulted in him going for and getting a role that he might not previously have considered or had the confidence to apply for. Having absolute clarity on what you have to offer and the value you bring are key to getting a new role. He has made a slight shift in his role type and is extremely happy with the new opportunity.

The next step is to consider your routes to the job market. You may want to utilise all of them or start with just a couple.

Looking for a new role can feel like a full-time job, particularly if you are still in a role, so you need to manage it carefully and not get burnt out or demotivated. Even if you are not in a role, it is best to structure your time and commit so many hours a day. You will be far more focused that way.

An obvious route to market is through recruiters and headhunters. It is better to select a few who are relevant for your work area and to spend time building relationships with them rather than firing off CVs in all directions. You may want to ask people you know for recommendations.

I would always recommend contacting them by phone first and having a discussion, following this up with a CV then keeping in touch with them regularly to build the relationship so they think of you when relevant opportunities do come up.

What you also need to do is be focused on what you are looking for with each recruiter. You may vary this slightly with different recruiters, but individuals need to have a very clear idea of your skills and what you want. It may work out that they present you with slightly different opportunities, acknowledging that they are different, but this won't happen at all if you are too vague. If you are considering different routes, it is often best to focus on one with a specific recruiter, at least initially.

Recruiters receive loads of CVs and have many conversations, so you need to think about how you can be positively memorable and clear about who you are and what you can offer. The more senior and/or specialised you get, the fewer recruiter options there are likely to be, which actually makes it easier – assuming you make a positive impact when you engage with them.

I don't typically recommend job boards as they usually involve sending off a CV and rarely hearing anything back, which can be demotivating. However, the 'Jobs' section on LinkedIn has some excellent roles and is a useful tool to save searches according to your criteria so you receive alerts. If you are not 100% sure what you are going for, then reviewing the job descriptions on LinkedIn can help you to shape what you apply for and what to include on your CV.

Approaching companies directly is another route. Many company websites feature roles they are looking to fill. I would approach this route by distilling the top five to ten companies you'd like to work for, with your criteria in mind, and then researching them. If there is nothing on their website, it can be helpful to use LinkedIn to find relevant people who work there. Connecting 'cold' is a bit risky, so a better option is to see whether anyone you know is connected to them and is prepared to introduce you.

The final key route is your network – and a very valuable one it can be too! Start by identifying people who know you and your work fairly well, and who have influence and connections. Try to arrange a conversation with your priority contacts from your list. Avoid saying you are looking for a new role as they may then not agree to talk, as they may feel under pressure to have a definite way to help you. Instead, position it as a general catch-up or say you are considering your career and would appreciate some of their input. This is now a very common way in which roles get filled and even created.

Impact at interview

Assuming you have created an excellent CV and LinkedIn profile, and have a clear and focused job search strategy, the interview invitations should arrive.

Many people feel daunted by an interview, but thinking of it as a conversation can help. You need to be right for the role, but the role also needs to be right for you – it isn't a one-sided transaction.

When you attend an interview, there are three key aspects to keep in mind: the content of your answers, the impact you have on the interviewer(s) and the rapport you build.

Be clear about why you want the role and able to demonstrate this credibly through knowledge about the company and the role while relating this to your own experience and skills.

In answering the questions, always consider what the interviewer really wants to know and how you can best showcase your skills and experience. A helpful framework for the examples you give is to first provide a bit of *Context* so the person knows what was happening and ideally how challenging a situation was. This should be followed by the *Action* you personally took – so describing what you did and therefore the skills you demonstrated. You should conclude with the *Result* (the CAR framework). Whenever possible, support this with specifics, including data. Remember they will only know what you tell them about your skills and experience.

Even if you are asked something where you provide a conceptual answer or some principles you would apply, try to support this with an example to show you have actually done this. If you haven't, take a similar example and adapt it to illustrate how you think and how you approach situations and challenges.

Whatever you recount to an interviewer, it needs to make sense for someone who wasn't there at the time (sounds obvious, I know) so consider carefully what they need to know for it to do so without there being too much detail. Look for signs in their body language that they understand and are engaged, or alternatively that you are saying too much or they are confused.

After you have been asked a question, it is absolutely fine to take a few seconds to consider your answer. You can even vocalise now and then that you are thinking about the best example or response to give. Most of all, make sure you answer the question you are asked, not the one you think you heard!

In terms of building rapport and impact, you need to consider carefully all that was covered in earlier chapters. If you are meeting in person, consider the impact you make on the person from the minute they see you. This could be in the reception area, or when they enter the room. Hopefully they will initiate some general conversation, so make sure you engage with it.

If you are being interviewed online, think about what the interview(s) will see – just the top half of you, limited body language and your background. Make sure you are confident in using the relevant technology; if you are struggling, this will impact your confidence and their perception of you – although, of course, internet problems are common and understandable.

Throughout, listen to what they say and show that you are listening. Your body language and the pace and clarity with which you speak are of paramount importance for building credibility and rapport. As well as factually looking at the skills and experience you have, the interviewer(s) will want to get a sense that you would be a good fit for their team and they could work with you.

Asking some questions at the end helps to show your interest. One of these could be about the next steps in the recruitment process, if you are successful, as well as the culture of the team and the key challenges for the organisation at the current time.

If you are not successful at interview, then try to get as much feedback as possible, as this will help you improve for the next opportunity.

Is your role right?

I had two careers before starting my business. It may be that you know you want a change or maybe you feel unfulfilled and you need to consider whether you should continue on your current path.

Wanting a change is rarely just about a better salary and package, although that might be the surface reason. It's usually related to unfulfilling work, feeling under-appreciated (usually related to poor relationships) or a lack of work–life balance.

For some people, a career change is the right move, but for many, changes in your current working patterns, skills and habits can dramatically improve how you feel about your work.

My best advice is to make some time to really think about what is and isn't going well at work. Then you can get a sense of whether smaller changes within your current career – such as moving organisation or even department, upskilling and/or working on your relationships and non-technical skills – could shift the situation.

You could do that work on your own, with the help of a trusted friend/colleague or with a career expert. I'd advise you to not rush into making a big change (it's easy to think things are better elsewhere) and to make some time for quality thinking.

Exercise recap

Resources webpage:
https://gettingonatwork.co.uk/bookresources

- *CV checklist:* Use this document to help you assess the strength of your current CV.

Points to remember

- Be ready to apply for opportunities that arise unexpectedly.
- Your CV needs to showcase who you are and what you have achieved, as well as providing 'hooks' so that people will want to interview you and learn more.
- Treat looking for a new role like another job, and manage your activity carefully.
- Your network is often a great resource for exploratory conversations and even job opportunities.

Further reflections

1. If you haven't looked for a new role for a long time, what do you need to work on to be prepared?
2. If you have been looking for a new role, at what stage is the process not working? Are you getting interviews but not getting offers, or are you not even getting interviews?

Conclusion

I hope you have enjoyed reading this book and that it has been thought-provoking. The skills I have covered are accessible to all professionals and, with thought and practice, can be developed and improved.

The main obstacle is often that so few people consider all these elements, never mind put them into practice consistently. Remember that while others can support you in your career, it is yours to drive and manage.

The two most common blockers are interrelated – focusing on your current job and the tasks you have to get done and not making the time to consider how to progress your career.

It is essential to consider these elements in terms of your life overall – the role you want work to play beyond earning your salary.

What's next for you?

Related to the two most common blockers, my suggestion is always to carve out some time to do some in-depth thinking and planning, then make career development time a regular diary commitment. If it is in there even for a short period each week, it is more likely to happen sometimes rather than not at all.

If you do this, you will build your self-awareness and be able to focus on what you need to do to perform even better in your current role and progress from where you are.

A first step could be to go back through this book and list the elements you need to consider, then prioritise them. As we explored at the start of the book, you need to build a plan of development aspects to work on that is manageable and keeps you motivated to continue. It may help to have someone to be accountable to for the career development work you are doing (depending on what profile you were in Gretchen Rubin's *Four Tendencies* model).

I talked about providing feedback to others. It is essential to take responsibility for getting regular feedback about yourself, both formal and informal, from different people – peers, seniors and even juniors. Always be sure you understand exactly what someone is telling you so you can reflect on it thoroughly and, where appropriate, take action. Don't be afraid to ask questions and request examples. Remember that you do need to filter feedback regarding its quality, and whether it is genuine or not. Feedback is an important input into your career development time.

When working with clients, I encourage them to keep notes on different reflections they have about their workplace and professional relationships, as well as various situations and what occurred. This is so that we can discuss them – otherwise details and important nuances are often lost. Doing this for yourself can help you reflect more deeply, and help you to identify patterns.

Positive career outcomes can happen 'by accident', but considering what you can do to shape your career is vital, while at the same time remembering that you can't control everything related to it.

After reading this book, you may feel that like me you want to make a career change. This may be a huge shift, like the one I made, or a smaller one. If that is the case, then try to be excited rather than afraid, and make a plan with simple steps to explore your thinking further.

Whether you are content where you are but want to improve your day-to-day working life, want to be promoted, want to make a lateral move (yes, they can be valuable too!) in your current organisation or in a new one, or want to make a bigger change, I hope you will take action and make career development time a new positive habit to improve how you undertake your current role and to help you navigate your career path.

Use this book both as a catalyst for the action you need to take and as a guide to which you can refer back on an ongoing basis to help you do that effectively. We all spend a lot of time at work, so make time to improve your day-to-day fulfilment and effectiveness and achieve all you want to in your career and your life.

Index

W